Mapping the Psyche

An Introduction to
Psychological Astrology

Volume 1: The Planets and the Zodiac Signs

Clare Martin

The Wessex Astrologer

Published in 2016 by
The Wessex Astrologer Ltd,
4A Woodside Road
Bournemouth
BH5 2AZ
www.wessexastrologer.com

© Clare Martin 2016

Clare Martin asserts the moral right to be recognised as
the author of this work.

Cover Design by Jonathan Taylor
Cover picture, *Emblema 5 Auri Potabilis Chimice Praeparati*
The tree of life and the influences of the heavens.
17th century engraving by Wolfgang Kilian (1581–1662), Augsburg
US National Library of the History of Medicine

A catalogue record for this book is available at The British Library

ISBN 9781910531167
Previous edition by the CPA Press (2007) 9781900869324

No part of this book may be reproduced or used in any form or by any
means without the written permission of the publisher.
A reviewer may quote brief passages.

Table of Contents

Introduction	v
Lesson 1: Introduction to the Planets	1
The Solar System	1
Planetary Symbols	6
Planetary Correspondences	10
Vertical Thinking	10
Lesson 2: The Cast of Characters	18
The Seven Planets of the Old World	19
The Sun	20
The Moon	27
Mercury	34
Lesson 3: Venus and Mars	40
Venus	41
Mars	47
Lesson 4: Jupiter and Saturn	52
Jupiter	54
Saturn	57
The Old World	60
Lesson 5: The Outer Planets	64
Uranus	68
Neptune	76
Pluto	84
Chiron	91
Lesson 6: Introduction to the Signs of the Zodiac	99
The Zodiac in Time	101
The Symbols for the Zodiac Signs	104
Planetary Rulers of the Signs	108
Planets in Exaltation, Detriment and Fall	109

Lesson 7: Constructing the Zodiac	**112**
Number Symbolism	112
The Tetractys as a Developmental Model	115
Polarity in the Birth Chart	117
Lesson 8: Modes and Elements	**123**
Modes: Cardinal, Fixed and Mutable signs	125
The Four Elements	132
Lesson 9: The Fire and Earth Signs	**143**
Aries	149
Leo	153
Sagittarius	157
Taurus	160
Virgo	166
Capricorn	172
Lesson 10: The Air and Water Signs	**172**
Gemini	180
Libra	182
Aquarius	188
Cancer	192
Scorpio	198
Pisces	203
Bibliography and Recommended Reading	209

Introduction

Astrology is a form of imagination emerging from nature and having direct relevance for everyday life. It is an applied poetics, a vision of life on earth stimulated by movements in the heavens, which can take us into areas of self-reflection as no other system of symbols and images can.[1]

Over the years of teaching introduction courses in astrology, I have often wondered why, in this day and age, when we should know better, so many of us continue to be drawn to astrology. When I ask a new group of students what brought them here at this time in their lives, I often get the impression that they have not chosen astrology but that it has chosen them. It is not uncommon to hear students say that they have been interested in astrology for years and, in a sense, have been resisting it for years, but have found that, in the end, it won't go away. And so we eventually find ourselves in a class, not really knowing what it will mean to us, if anything, or where it will take us, because something in us has decided that it is time to learn.

These classes are for that 'something' in us which I have gradually come to think of as a kind of shamanic calling. Could it be that astrologers are actually 'chosen for their role by the spirits of the universe'?[2] Certainly, many of us have experienced the standard signatures of the shamanic calling: that astrology comes upon us in spite of ourselves; that we often attempt to avoid making a commitment to astrology, for the very good reason that astrology is a demanding vocation which we sense will change our lives forever; that as we become mediators between the worlds, with one foot in the other realms, we can no longer live fully in the world. Ultimately astrology is not a technique but an initiation into a way of life which, because of its mysterious familiarity, often feels like a coming home.

> Astrology is 'a saving kind of knowledge, an apprehension of the mysteries which run deep in nature and in the individual, a transforming knowledge which can only be acquired through learning that is far beyond intellect alone.[3]

Astrology and psychological astrology are difficult to define exactly. Perhaps astrology can best be described as a mythical and magical language and, as with all languages, every astrologer will develop their own way of interpreting and communicating its meaning. This course draws primarily on the work of C. G. Jung, who has given us a particular vocabulary which enables us to restore astrology to what I believe to be its rightful place, as one of the four great pillars of western esotericism, along with kabbalah, alchemy and magic.[4] In the esoteric traditions, the universe is perceived as 'an organic, alive and sacred whole, in which everything is woven together in one cosmic web, where all orders of manifest and unmanifest life are related, because all share in the sanctity of the original source'.[5]

For psychological astrologers the relationship between astrology and alchemy seems to be particularly significant. Historically, these twin sciences were not only strongly linked, but inseparable. The alchemists were practical people, and their approach is useful for the psychological astrologer since it encourages our active participation and personal engagement with the natal chart. In other words, there is a job to be done.

The basis of alchemy is that nature, and natural man, are not created perfect. In our original state, we are 'a confusion of spirit, soul and body', unconscious of ourselves to a large degree, and therefore, according to Jung, capable only of collective functioning. The astrological birth chart remains exactly the same for our entire lives. There is no guarantee that we will be any more integrated, evolved, or conscious by the time we die than when we were born. In our natural state we live under the sometimes tyrannical dominion of the planets. But what we do with our birth chart, and how we choose to live it, is up to us. A psychological approach works against our natural state in the service of increasing consciousness.

The alchemists were deliberately working against the natural order of things by helping nature do what she could not do for herself.

> Nature does not produce anything that is perfect in itself; man must bring things to their perfection – this work is called 'alchemy'... Things are created and given into our hands, but not in the ultimate form that is proper to them... In the seed is inherent from the beginning the purpose and function... For alchemy means: to

carry to its end something that has not yet been completed; to obtain the lead from the ore and to transform it into what it is made for.[6]

Alchemy is fundamentally optimistic. 'The *opus alchemicum* not only changes, perfects or redeems Nature, but also brings to perfection human existence'.[7]

Like the alchemist and the magician, the psychological astrologer participates actively in a dialogue with nature. A psychological approach is not unlike the 'great work' or *magnum opus* of the alchemists. Both involve a careful and deliberate cooperation in the task of creating consciousness. This is no easy option since it involves prolonged periods of self analysis, the courage to confront and integrate our own hidden darknesses, to recognise our self righteousness, defensiveness and deepest fears, and the decision to take personal responsibility for ourselves, rather than being content to live as passive victims of what we suppose to be our pre-determined 'fate'.

> The process of psychological differentiation is no light work; it needs the tenacity and patience of the alchemist, who must purify the body from all superfluities in the fiercest heat of the furnace.[8]

The illusion that all our problems are caused by outside forces or can be blamed, for example, on our birth charts comes to an end when we start to take back our projections and to look at things from within. The process of *individuation*, of 'deliberately working against the natural order of things', leads to the creation of what Jung called the 'Self', an internal structure which gives us a 'feeling of standing on solid ground, on a patch of inner eternity which even physical death cannot touch'.

The magnum opus had two aims: 'the rescue of the human soul and the salvation of the cosmos'.[10] This means that, however small and unimportant our individual efforts may seem, we will nevertheless be playing our own small part in helping nature do what she is unable to do for herself:

> Once a vision of life as an organic whole is accepted in principle, humanity becomes in one sense a co-creator with nature, in so far as it can foster, ignore or destroy its identity with nature, for nature's continued existence depends ultimately on the kind of consciousness we bring to bear on it.[11]

Notes
1. Thomas Moore, *The Re-Enchantment of Everyday Life*.
2. Caitlin Matthews, *Singing the Soul Back Home: Shamanic Wisdom for Every Day*.
3. Frances A. Yates, description of Hermetic knowledge in *Giordano Bruno and the Hermetic Tradition*.
4. Thorwald Dethlefsen, *The Challenge of Fate*, p.13.
5. Anne Baring and Jules Cashford, *The Myth of the Goddess*, Preface, p.xi.
6. Paracelsus, quoted in *Inner Alchemy*, Parabola, Volume III, Number 3.
7. Mircea Eliade, *Inner Alchemy*, Parabola, Volume III, Number 3
8. C. G. Jung, *The Psychology of the Transference*, p.132.
9. Marie Louise von Franz, *C.G. Jung, His Myth in Our Time*.
10. C. G. Jung Speaking in a 1952 interview, Eranos Foundation.
11. A. Baring and Jules Cashford, *The Myth of the Goddess*, p.681.

LESSON 1

Introduction to the Planets

The Solar System

The astrological tradition is thousands of years old, originating from the meticulous observations and careful recordings by the Mesopotamian priest/astrologers of the ever-changing positions of the seven planets visible to the naked eye, both in relation to each other and against the backdrop of the stars and constellations. A 'horoscope' (or *time map*) is a representation of the positions of the planets as viewed from the Earth at a particular time and place on Earth. Astrology has always been and remains a geocentric system since, although the Sun is in the centre of the solar system, the Earth is nevertheless our home, and it is from the Earth that we take our bearings.

Audience: So it was basic observation and record keeping which was the origin of astrology in the first place?

Clare: That's right. Mesopotamia has always been referred to as the birthplace of western civilisation, and it was here that the art, craft and science of western astrology was first forged. Mesopotamia is a largely flat desert land with wide horizons and huge night skies. It is therefore not surprising that the first myths are often celestial stories or that the heavenly bodies were considered to be deities – living powers whose relationship to human beings was both obvious and taken for granted. Now that we no longer look upwards or watch the planets moving through the night skies we have lost our instinctive connection to these living gods and collectively we have ceased to take astrology seriously. It is sometimes said that the planets have stopped speaking to us because we have stopped listening to them, but if you have ever been in a place far from anywhere and looked up at the night sky, you will have experienced something of the majesty and power of the stars and planets.

If there is any spark of imagination left in us, as we stand beneath the stars, trusting the emotions and intuitions that rise up in us, we can feel with bodily certainty that these birds of fire have an impact on human life, an influence that is undeniable.[1]

As students of astrology, one of our first tasks is to get to know and understand the very basic astronomy and mechanics of the solar system. This is the foundation of our art and of our craft and if you can learn this now, it will stand you in good stead throughout your astrological studies. So let's look at the order of the planets from the Sun. The anatomy of our solar system is not necessarily well understood. But it is extremely important for us, as astrologers, to know, not only because an understanding of the orbit periods of the planets and of their relative speeds is crucial when we come to study the planetary cycles and forecasting techniques, but also because the physical characteristics of the planets tell us a great deal about their astrological meaning.

So we see from the following diagram that the orbital periods of the planets depends on their distance from the Sun. The first planet out from the Sun is Mercury, which moves very quickly, with an orbital period of only 88 days. Most of the time Mercury is obscured from view since it is either in front of or behind the Sun. When we do see it, it is only for a brief period as it darts round the outside of the Sun, now one side, now the other. Even the astronomy of the planets can tell us something about their astrological personality. Venus has an orbit of 225 days and has always been known as the Morning Star when it rises with the Sun in the east, and as the Evening Star when it sets with the Sun in the west, representing two faces of this great goddess. Mercury and Venus are known as 'inferior' planets, since their orbits lie inside the orbit of the Earth. Because of this, they appear to accompany the Sun on its annual journey around the birth chart, sometimes ahead of and sometimes lagging behind the Sun, with Mercury never further than 27° and Venus never further than 48° from the Sun.

The Earth's orbit falls outside Venus and, as we know, its apparent orbit around the Sun takes 365.25 days, or a year. The Moon is the Earth's satellite and takes approximately 28–29 days to orbit the Earth. New Moons occur every month (or 'moonth'), when the Moon is between the Earth and the Sun, and full Moons occur every month, when the Earth is between the Moon and the Sun, as in the diagram.

Introduction to the Planets   3

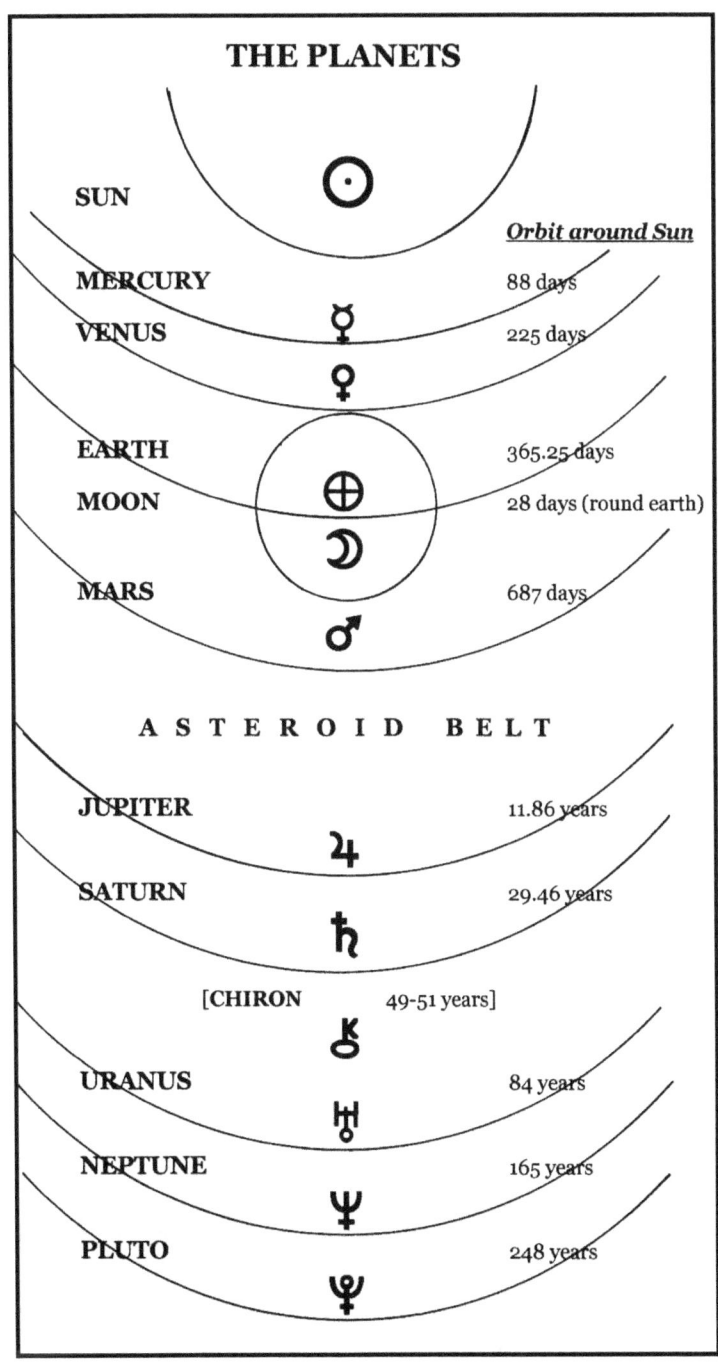

Mars is the first 'superior' planet, lying outside the orbit of the Earth, and takes 687 days, or roughly two years, to orbit the Sun. With its red colour, it has always been associated with bloodshed, anger and war, and with its two satellites Phobos and Daimos (meaning 'terror' and 'fear') it is known as the god of war. With its extremely elliptical orbit, Mars appears to grow in size and power as it advances towards the Earth and is at its closest when the Earth is between the Sun and Mars. It then appears to retreat until it reaches its furthest distance from the Earth, on the other side of the Sun. Known as the god Ares by the Greeks, the Roman month of March (when the Sun is in the sign of Aries) was named after this planet.

Outside the orbit of Mars lies the asteroid belt, a wide belt of rocks, considered by some to be the fragmented remains of an exploded planet. The asteroid belt is an astrologically significant boundary, since it marks the division between the five 'personal' planets (Sun, Moon, Mercury, Venus and Mars) and the two 'social' planets (Jupiter and Saturn). The personal planets describe our individual characteristics, whereas the social planets describe how each of us relates to the wider social and cultural context into which we are born.

Jupiter, with an orbital period of 11.86 years, is the largest planet in the solar system, ten times the size of the earth. With its huge magnetic field, it radiates more energy into space than it receives from the Sun. With its family of moons, permanent storms, great red spot and axial rotation of about ten hours, everything about Jupiter is active, turbulent, stormy and larger than life.

Saturn, with an orbital period of 29.46 years, is second largest planet and its icy, clear, ring system makes it one of the most beautiful objects in the solar system. As the furthermost and slowest planet visible to the naked eye, Saturn remains the outer planet in the solar system from the point of view of our senses, and this fact, together with its perfect ring system, has meant that Saturn has always been associated with boundaries and time, and the limitations of our existence. Psychologically, Saturn is related to the development of strong ego boundaries, which keep us safe, but which also confine and restrict us.

The 'trapped asteroid' or 'planetoid' Chiron was first discovered in 1977 and remains a misfit in the solar system. Originating from the Kuiper Belt, which lies outside the orbit of Pluto, it is not known how long this visitor to our solar system will remain with us. With an extremely elliptical orbit of 49–51 years, Chiron's astrological function appears to be to link the outer planets with the 'old world' planets, since it fluctuates almost as far from the Sun as Uranus, and yet it passes within the orbital sphere of Saturn. Although Chiron has by no means been universally accepted into astrological lore, I want to include it from the beginning because, as a psychological principle, it appears to be particularly relevant to us in this particular period in history.

The three outer planets, Uranus, Neptune and Pluto, belong to a very different order indeed. Their discovery was only made possible through the development of scientific instruments, such as the telescope, and appears to reflect a corresponding expansion of human awareness and consciousness. The discovery of Uranus in 1781 doubled the size of the solar system overnight and shattered the old world view – a profoundly shocking, unexpected and exciting development, which immediately tells us something about its astrological interpretation. Neptune's discovery in 1846 and Pluto's discovery in 1930 have heralded the current era, with all its tremendous potential for collective evolution and collective destruction.

Audience: There is a lot to learn, isn't there?

Clare: Yes. Learning astrology is very similar to embarking on an apprenticeship. Astrology is a practical craft which cannot be mastered 'with the head' only. We each need to find our own unique relationship to astrology and our hard work and dedication is repaid when we find ourselves tapping into the living astrological tradition, at which point the subject, and each chart we study, begins to come alive for us. It is the apprenticeship which prepares us for this magical moment, when we first find ourselves in a dialogue with the living cosmos.

Mapping the Psyche 1: The Planets and the Zodiac Signs

Planetary Symbols

Clare: Although we can learn something about the astrological meaning of the planets from their physical position in the solar system, the planetary symbols themselves are also extremely revealing. It is important to get to know these symbols, since they are part of the language of astrology, and by practising drawing them – when you are on the bus or on the telephone – will help you to make them yours. As we develop our own relationship to the planets we also develop our own particular writing style for the symbols.

The planetary symbols, or glyphs, are derived from a combination of the symbols for spirit, soul and matter, from which all life is said to derive in varying proportions. Their essential meanings can be found by analysing their individual components:

○ The circle – long considered to be the most perfect shape of all – is an image of pure spirit.

∪ The crescent is the symbol for the soul, which can be seen, as here, reaching upwards towards spirit, or as in the symbol for the Moon reaching 'backwards' towards the past, or both backwards and forwards in the symbol for the planet Uranus.

| The vertical line is the symbol for mind

— The horizontal line is the symbol for body

+ When the mind and body are combined, they form the cross of matter.

Symbols are complicated things since, as Jung observed, they can never be fully interpreted – they can only be experienced. Symbols transcend the split between the rational and the irrational, the known and the unknown.

Sun and Moon

The symbol for the Sun is pure spirit with the dot of consciousness in the centre. The symbol for the Moon is pure soul, with two – or sometimes three – arcs reaching 'backwards' towards the past. It is symbolically significant that, in neither case, is the cross of matter present.

Earth

The Earth is the planet on which our lives become manifest, and the cross of matter is placed in the centre, surrounded by the circle of spirit, within which all life is contained.

Mercury

Mercury contains all the symbols, signifying the potential integration of spirit, soul and matter and the synthesis of all the other planets, as well as the relationships between them. Soul – the mediating and connecting principle – is in the most elevated position, above the spirit, with matter at the base.

Venus and Mars

Venus and Mars symbolise the physical manifestations of the male/female polarity in the world. Originally, the symbol for Mars was the cross of matter above the circle of spirit, and the symbols therefore complement each other, with Venus elevating spirit over matter and Mars elevating matter over spirit. In neither case is the symbol for the soul present.

Jupiter and Saturn

The symbols for the next pair of planets, Jupiter and Saturn, concern the relationship between the soul and body. With Jupiter, the soul is elevated over the cross of matter, signifying the importance of finding a meaningful connection (soul), 'something to live for' in the manifest world. Jupiter frees the soul from the dominance of matter. With Saturn, the cross of matter is elevated over the soul, signifying that the soul's yearnings must be given shape and form within the limitations of existence in time and space.

Uranus, Neptune and Pluto

Uranus shows the cross of matter bracketed by two vertical lines of mind, over a small circle of spirit indicating the power of the mind to harness natural forces. An alternative symbol for Uranus replaces the two vertical lines of mind with two arcs of soul facing away from each other, one towards the past and one towards the future, harnessed by the cross of matter between them. Neptune is the crescent of soul impaled upon the cross of matter. Soul reaches upwards but is penetrated – or trapped – by matter. The symbol for Neptune, therefore, could be said to portray the soul's suffering while it is encased in matter, and its longing to return to its source – the spirit. Pluto is a composite of all three symbols – the crescent of the soul enclosing a small circle of spirit, with the cross of matter below. Spirit could be said to dominate matter through the medium of the soul. An alternative explanation is that this symbol is a combination of the letters P and L, the initials of Percival Lowell, its discoverer.

Chiron

There are two possible explanations for this symbol. The first is to interpret the symbol above the circle simply as the letter K, after Charles Koval, the astronomer who first discovered Chiron's presence in the solar system. Alternatively, we could interpret this as the vertical line of mind, from which two diagonal lines emerge, one moving upwards and the other moving downwards. The diagonal lines could represent the combined, integrated horizontal/vertical body/mind, reaching upwards towards the heavens and downwards towards the Earth.

Audience: I can understand that the combination of mind and body makes the cross of matter and describes manifestation – or something real and tangible in this world, but I am not so clear how spirit and soul come into the picture – or what the difference is between them?

Clare: This is a huge question and, of course, very relevant from the point of view of astrology's roots in the ancient mystery traditions. Although the birth chart describes our manifest lives in space and time, it always fascinates me that the great mysteries of the spirit and the soul always seem to hover in the background as we study and practice astrology, however pragmatic our approach. Jung observed that the spirit and the soul are present in all cultures, religions and languages but, being symbols of essence, they are almost impossible to define exactly.[2] The Greek word *anemos* ('wind') refers to the 'breath of life' and from this root are derived the two Latin words *Animus* 'spirit' and *Anima* 'soul'. This tells us that spirit and soul share the same source but, as James Hillman points out, 'the ways of the soul and those of the spirit only sometimes coincide'.[3] Rather, they reflect a fundamental tension in human life. Spirit and soul are symbols like yang and yin, representing two slants on life, two perspectives.

By analogy, spirit and soul are related to each other as the Sun is to the Moon and as masculine is to feminine, as Logos is to Eros, as Apollonian is to Dionysian, polarities which are reflected within every birth chart. The world of spirit, like the Sun, is 'transcendent, blazing with light and fire'.[4] Spirit is 'superior', masculine, conscious, rational, transcendent, clear. It is the 'highest goal of all development and evolution, and the ground of all life, as present fully in the beginning as in the end'.[5]

The world of soul, or psyche, on the other hand, can be found in the diffuse impressions lying beneath the surface of everyday experience. Soul is vulnerable, it remembers and suffers. Soul is 'inferior', feminine, unconscious, dark, immanent. The soul is the mediating principle between the world of spirit and the realm of matter. Without soul there would be no connection between the spirit and the world.

Planetary Correspondences

According to the 'perennial philosophy', the universe is a living pattern, or network of fields of resonance vibrating at different frequencies in the great chain of creation.[6] Everything in the universe is perceived as vibrating in descending frequency from the level of spirit to soul, mind, body and matter, which includes the various frequencies of the animal and plant worlds, as well as the densest frequencies of the colours, metals, minerals and stones. Each field or level of resonance in the 'hierarchy of creation' is reflected in every other field, an understanding common to all the mystery traditions and central to astrology. The tree of life in the kabbalah is also a reflection of this scheme, and if you are interested in these ideas, then I recommend that you read the books of Warren Kenton (Z'ev ben Shimon Halevi).

Vertical Thinking

Astrologers are, by nature, vertical thinkers. Vertical thinking adds another dimension to the more familiar horizontal thinking which is so favoured in our western educational system and culture. It enables us to identify the sympathetic correspondences which exist between various different fields of resonance. Seemingly unrelated objects and events immediately fall into a living relationship with each other, making connections which often explain the way we have instinctively felt about the world.

Have a look at the Table of Planetary Correspondences. Find the Plant World category on the left hand side of the page and read horizontally across the page. Now most people will immediately see the connection between marigolds and cauliflowers, medicinal herbs, cultivated crops, nettles, onions, maple trees, hemlock and orchids, wouldn't they? They all belong to the plant world category which is familiar to us. Equally, if you follow the Mineral World category horizontally, you will find gold, silver, mercury, copper, iron, tin, lead, etc. The connection is obvious.

Now let's look at the same chart vertically. Now we are identifying the sympathetic correspondences which exist between the various

TABLE OF PLANETARY CORRESPONDENCES

	SUN	MOON
Zodiac Sign	Leo	Cancer
House Ruler	5th	4th
Mundane	Empires, kingdoms, theatres, palaces, mansions, places of entertainment, casinos, showboats, solariums, gold mines, fireplaces.	Homes – children's and old people's, hotels, taverns, houseboats, aquariums, ponds, restaurants, bakeries, beaches, boats, boathouses.
People	Men generally, royalty, emperors, courtiers, heads of states, presidents, patrons, figureheads, actors, film 'stars', celebrities, heart specialists, goldsmiths.	Women generally, relatives, families, cooks and caterers, hoteliers, housewives, midwives, fishermen, crowds.
Body	Heart, back, spinal column.	Breasts, stomach, bladder, bowels, womb, tears, lymph system, bodily fluids, gastric juices, saliva, sleep.
Animal World	Lions, peacocks.	Nocturnal animals and birds, owls, domestic fowl, clams, coral, fish, frogs, tortoises, turtles, snails, shellfish, crabs.
Plant World	Heliotropes, marigolds, sunflowers, golden or large & showy flowers, oranges, saffron, nutmeg.	Watery fruits, cauliflowers, cabbages, cucumbers, daisies, dew, white or night-blooming flowers, fungus, water plants, water lilies, turnips, trees rich in sap, seaweed.
Mineral World	Gold.	Silver, pearls.
Colour	Gold, orange, saffron.	Silver, white, grey.

	MERCURY	VENUS
Zodiac Sign	Gemini & Virgo	Taurus & Libra
House Ruler	3rd & 6th	2nd & 7th
Mundane	Schools, shops, markets, fairs, tennis courts, roads, cars, bicycles, garages, telephones, diaries, keys, newspapers, stationery, books, filing & medicine cabinets.	Gardens, wardrobes, dressing tables, art galleries, concert halls, beauty parlours, boutiques, brothels, casinos, vineyards, embassies, dating agencies, social functions, weddings.
People	Tradesmen, secretaries, journalists, taxi & bus drivers, couriers, forgers, graphologists, printers, interpreters, jugglers, critics, teachers, shop assistants, auditors, bookkeepers, pharmacists, computer programmers, craftsmen, dieticians, hygienists, librarians, proof-readers, surveyors, watchmakers.	Musicians, artists, jewelers, models, bankers, diplomats, receptionists, beauty consultants, make-up artists, manicurists, milliners, tailors, architects, divorce lawyers, farmers.
Body	Brain, hands, lungs, arms, digestive & nervous systems, intestines, circulation, co-ordination, respiratory system.	Neck, throat, thyroid gland, kidneys, venous blood.
Animal World	Small animals generally, butterflies, birds, bees, monkeys, parrots, carrier pigeons.	Cattle, farm animals, domesticated animals.
Plant World	Medicinal herbs, small plants.	Cultivated crops, flowers and fruit generally, apples, roses, blossom, vines.
Mineral World	Quicksilver (Mercury)	Brass, bronze, copper, precious stones & gems.
Colour	Many colours together, white and pale blue (Virgo).	Pale blue and pink, earth colours (Taurus).

Introduction to the Planets

	MARS	JUPITER
Zodiac Sign	Aries & Scorpio	Sagittarius & Pisces
House Ruler	1st & 8th	9th & 12th
Mundane	Battlefields, fire stations, forges, foundries, furnaces, fires, weapons, knives, guns, cutting & drilling instruments, dental drills, incinerators, military bases & barracks, slaughterhouses.	Courts, churches, colleges, universities, embassies, pageants, jousts, parades, public functions, pulpits, religious organisations, racing stables, long distance travel, passports.
People	Soldiers, firemen, athletes, metal workers, carpenters, surgeons, dentists, martial artists.	Lawyers, barristers, benefactors, university dons & lecturers, philosophers, clergymen, missionaries, explorers, foreigners, horse trainers, jockeys, veterinarians.
Body	Head, adrenal glands & adrenalin, iron in the blood, muscles, spots & pimples, rashes, excretory system & organs, genitals, testicles.	Thighs, liver.
Animal World	Rams, birds of prey, stinging insects, scorpions, snakes, eagles.	Large animals generally, elephants, racehorses, horses generally, animals with valuable fur.
Plant World	Nettles, radishes, spices, thorn-bearing plants, arsenic, capers, cayenne, garlic, horseradish, mustard, onions, witch hazel.	Clover, maple trees.
Mineral World	Iron, brimstone, garnet.	Tin.
Colour	Red and black.	Royal blue, purple.

	SATURN	**URANUS**
Zodiac Sign	**Capricorn & Aquarius**	**Aquarius**
House Ruler	10th & 11th	11th
Mundane	Mountains, deserts, graveyards, corpses, cells, caves, prisons, walls, barriers, dams, ruins, beards, boulders, bricks, stone mills, cement, handcuffs, mortgages	Television stations, satellites, electricity, radio waves, computers, the internet, new technology, laser beams, magnetic fields, telepathy, air conditioners, ice, icebergs, glaciers.
People	Old people, those in authority, civil service, administrators, engineers, mathematicians, builders, chimney sweeps, mineralogists, archivists, coroners, funeral directors, historians, gaolers.	Scientists, astronomers, astrologers, radiographers, inventors, revolutionaries, anarchists, politicians, archaeologists, pilots.
Body	Bones, cartilage, skin, gall bladder, teeth, knees, kneecaps.	Ankles.
Animal World	Animals with protective armour, beasts of burden, horned animals, burrowing animals and reptiles, camels, animals feeding on carrion, mountain goats.	
Plant World	Hemlock, ivy, cyprus, elm & poplar trees.	Orchids.
Mineral World	Lead, diamonds, marble, coal, crystals.	Uranium, platinum.
Colour	Black, dark brown, grey, flat or dark colours.	Electric blue.

	NEPTUNE	PLUTO
Zodiac Sign	Pisces	Scorpio
House Ruler	12th	8th
Mundane	Hospitals, prisons, breweries, convents, monasteries, pilgrims, holy relics, the sea, oil, floods, alcohol, drugs & poisons, anaesthetics, fashion, religion.	Underground transport, sewers, power stations, volcanoes, earthquakes, secret societies, political underground.
People	Dancers, artists, actors, illusionists, photographers, poets, filmmakers, priests, fishmongers, chiropodists, reflexologists.	Psychiatrists, analysts, pathologists, liquidators, sewerage workers, waste recyclers, detectives, secret police, potholers.
Body	Feet.	Sexual organs, bodily elimination.
Animal World	Marine life, fish.	Snake, scorpion, eagle.
Plant World	Water lily, willow.	Rhododendron, deep-rooted plants.
Mineral World	Neptunium.	Plutonium.
Colour	Soft sea-green.	Dark red, maroon.

different fields of resonance. Starting at the foot of the Sun column, the Sun resonates to the mineral gold and to the colour gold. Moving up to the plant world, the solar plants are marigolds and sunflowers, which are heliotropic, following the Sun's path during the day. The orange is a solar fruit, and it follows that eating oranges will increase your vitality, or solar energy. These correspondences are central to the traditions of herbal medicine and healing and if you can find an original copy of *Culpeper's Herbal*, you will find lists of herbs and plants which heal the diseases relating to the various planets. In holistic healing practices these correspondences are real, and not just symbolic. In the animal world, the lion is a solar creature, the 'golden maned' lion, the 'pride' of lions. The regal nature of the lion corresponds to the solar principle. One level up again, we see that the Sun rules the heart, the back and the spinal column, which is also associated with pride and with holding one's head high, another solar correspondence.

Moving up another level, each planet rules groups or types of people. As the masculine principle, the Sun rules men in general, royalty, film stars and anyone at the centre of attention, a reflection of the fact that the Sun is at the centre of our solar system. The solar function is visibility, to shine boldly and brightly and to draw attention. Additionally, solar professions such as a goldsmith belong in this category. Each planet also rules a particular aspect of the mundane world – 'mundus' meaning world. The Sun rules palaces and theatres, buildings which are designed to reflect the glory of the central players, whose function is to bask in the limelight.

One of the main goals of this term is to start building a planetary vocabulary, since there are many words and other associations for each of the planets right through the different levels. As we have seen, the solar principle describes lions, palaces, gold, sunflowers and kings, but it also describes psychological qualities of confidence, enthusiasm and radiance. It is the symbol for spirit, it is about focus, daylight, clarity and authority. Exactly the same kinds of connections exist for all the planets, and as we explore each of the planets it is worth referring to this chart for the various associations at different levels, so that you can begin to build a rich and comprehensive vocabulary around each of them.

Audience: What should we read to prepare for next week?

Clare: Well, we have been doing the basics today, and I would really like you to learn the order of the planets, their orbit times, and the planetary symbols. Test yourself and write the planetary symbols whenever you have a few moments. This is a very good way to start making your own unique relationship with the planets.

The Scheme of the Universe [7]
The individual is portrayed as a microcosm of the unity of the cosmos

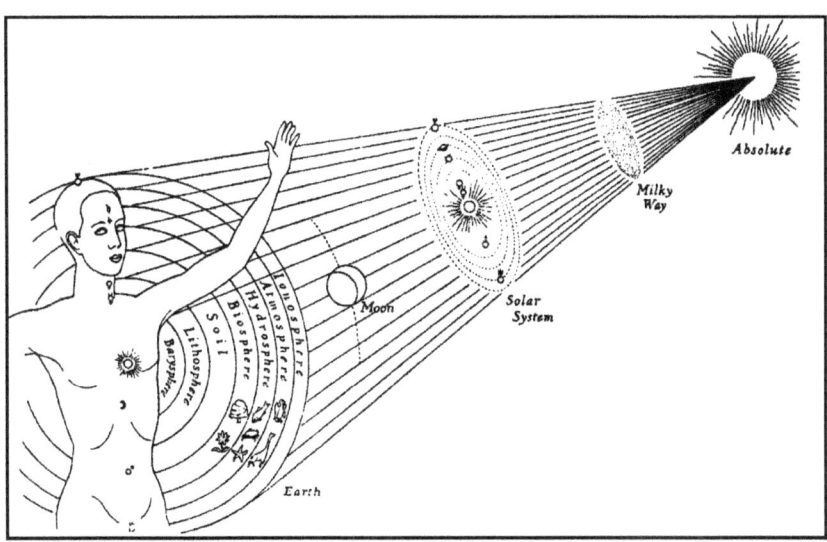

Notes
1. Thomas Moore, *The Re-Enchantment of Everyday Life*, p.315.
2. C.G. Jung, *The Structure and Dynamics of the Psyche*.
3. Thomas Moore (ed.) *The Essential James Hillman: A Blue Fire*.
4. Thomas Moore (ed.) op.cit.
5. Ken Wilber, *The Eye of Spirit*, Chapter 1: The Spectrum of Consciousness.
6. Ken Wilber: op.cit.
7. Rodney Collin, *The Theory of Celestial Influence: Man, the Universe and Cosmic Mystery*.

LESSON 2

The Cast of Characters

Each one of us is a reflection of the entire cosmos as it exists in space and time at the moment of our birth. This means that each one of us contains the pattern of the entire cosmos within. The archetypal,[1] or universal, symbolism of each planet is modified and personalised according to its placement in our birth charts. In this way, the planets will function as a unique, personalised, cast of characters. Each planet has its own personality, motivation, attitude, desires, goals and expressions, right down to its own way of walking and talking, its own body posture and the particular clothes it wears! Roberto Assagioli, the founder of Psychosynthesis, believed that we each contain a multiplicity of selves, or 'sub-personalities'.[2] 'Each of us is a crowd ... and in every corner of my soul there is an altar to a different god.' The problem, as Jung pointed out, is how to find ourselves in the crowd.[3]

The astrologer's task is to assess how the archetypal meaning – or 'eternal pattern' – has become modified and personalised for each individual. This careful analysis lies at the heart of the art and craft of psychological astrology, with its goal of promoting self awareness and psychic integration, since almost invariably, at least a few of our planets, or sub-personalities, will have become distorted along the way, and will be functioning in a negative, defensive or self-destructive way, or will have fallen into the unconscious so that we are unaware of the power they hold over us. We need to honour all the planetary gods on their own terms, lay our offerings on the steps of each of their temples in order to appease them and gain their support.

The psychological astrologer attempts to identify which planets may have become distorted or degraded. It is possible to enter into a dialogue with all the planets in order to promote a deeper, more profound and empowering relationship to them. At the core of each planet lies its pure archetypal quality, along with vital and creative elements of our being. We do have the potential to access the 'gifts of the planetary gods', however negative they may seem to us at first.

The Seven Planets of the Old World

Until the discovery of the three outer planets, astrology was concerned only with the seven planets visible to the naked eye. With the exception of Mercury, these planets can be usefully studied as three pairs of opposites. We will begin with the two luminaries – the Sun and Moon – which, in astrological terminology, are known as planets.

Essentially, the Sun and Moon represent our personal connection to spirit and soul, as can be seen clearly from the symbols for each planet. Neither symbol contains the cross of matter, which means that, ultimately, neither the spirit nor the soul belongs exclusively to our manifest lives, but to other realms of existence. During our lifetimes, however, which are the concern of our birth charts, the principles of spirit and soul are, as it were, 'stepped down' and projected onto our experience of our human parents, father and mother, creators of our physical existence.

The astrological Sun and Moon oppose and complement each other, respectively ruling the day and the night, light and darkness, male and female, action and receptivity, clarity and complexity, radiating and reflecting qualities, certainty and doubt, straightness and roundness, and many other opposites associated with the opposing male and female principles.

Every chart contains both the Sun and Moon which reveals, as Jung observed, that within the psyche the masculine and feminine principles are equally represented. It is never possible to know the gender of an individual from their birth chart, since the chart is simply the map of a particular moment in time and space and does not belong solely to us as individuals. Rather, the birth chart describes how the masculine and feminine principles will function in an individual's life, regardless of their gender. This is an important point, because in these politically correct times, people often have initial difficulty appreciating that the analogies drawn in astrology between masculine/feminine, positive/negative, active/passive, yang/yin, do not refer to our biology but to our psyches, which contain a potential balance between these opposites.

20 Mapping the Psyche 1: The Planets and the Zodiac Signs

An engraving from Michael Maier's alchemical text, *Atalanta fugiens*, (1618), showing the Sun and Moon as the twin complementary principles of the alchemical work.

SUN

Astronomically, the Sun is at the centre, or heart, of the solar system. Without the Sun, there would be no light or life and, indeed, no solar system. The Sun in the birth chart represents our centre of gravity and our centre of consciousness. When the Sun is shining, all is well with the world. Did anyone experience the total solar eclipse in Plymouth in 1999?

Audience: Yes, and it was a very bizarre thing. It was a gloomy day and cloudy, and as it gradually got darker I kept thinking 'this is it', and then it was suddenly night. Not the gradual fading of the light, like sunset, but sudden – the light just disappeared. It was very creepy. But I found the most significant thing was when the Sun appeared again after a few

The Cast of Characters 21

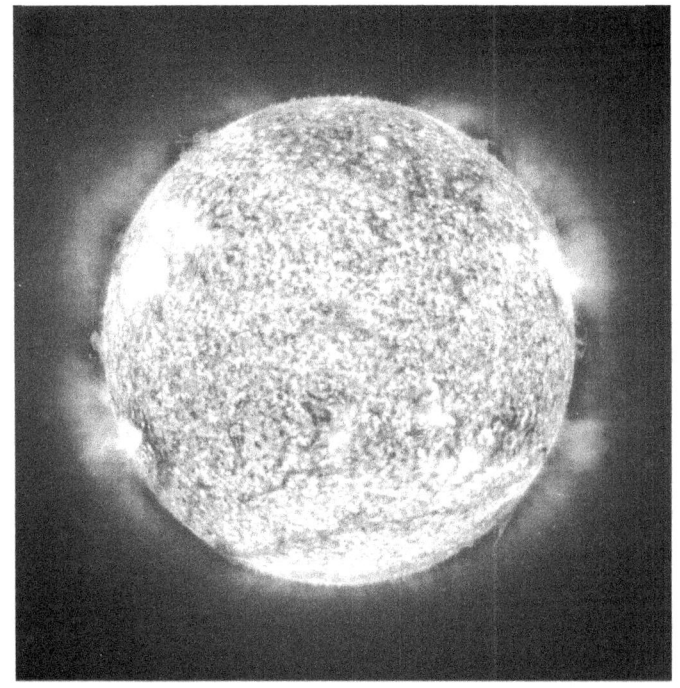

minutes – my heart just lifted up, and it was just a really good feeling about being there.

Clare: That's very interesting, since you mentioned the lifting of your heart, and the Sun rules the heart.

Audience: Yes, it was definitely my heart.

Clare: There is also a spiritual component to what you say. We take the Sun for granted, and it is only when it dies that we appreciate how everything depends on it. With the return of the Sun everything has meaning and purpose and everything is alright again. The wondrous light comes back. I gather that during a solar eclipse everything on the Earth stops growing and literally starts to die, including us, so it is fortunate that they only last for about four minutes or so.

Audience: It was very quiet. The birds stopped singing.

Clare: Astrologically, the Sun describes the masculine principle, reliable, predictable, direct and focussed, the source of our vitality and spiritual identity. Every day the Sun rises in the east, restoring light and confidence and clarity and the life force to the Earth. Equally, the heat and dryness of this solar principle can burn and scorch and can be extremely dangerous, to the extent that we cannot even look at the Sun directly with the naked eye. The Sun describes what we already are in essence, but what will take the conscious striving of our life's journey to make whole and to integrate.

Arrogance, haughtiness, pride and narcissism, for example, are a few examples of the distortion of the solar principle, the archetype of nobility, honour, integrity and personal authority. As we work to develop the solar principle, which is ultimately our conscious connection to Spirit, we learn that the full expression of the Sun involves the integration of the shadow, since there can be no light without a shadow. The achievement of our unique identity, or solar 'individuality' therefore implies that we have become 'un-divided', we have recognised and integrated both the light and dark aspects of our solar nature. Naturally, this is very difficult to do and takes a lifetime's work.

There are two particularly appropriate Greek myths which describe the dangers of trying to harness the Sun's power too young. This is an act of hubris, an identification with the gods, and is always punished. One is the myth of Phaeton, son of the sun-god Helios, who induced his father to allow him to drive the chariot of the sun across the heavens for one day. The horses, feeling their reins held by an inexperienced hand, ran

In Salomon Trismosin's alchemical text, *Splendor solis* (1582), the purified Cosmic Sun, rising from the darkness, conjoins with the Earth at the end of the alchemical work: "that which is above unites with that which is below", symbolising on a psychological level the integration of the whole personality.

wildly out of their course and came close to the Earth threatening to burn it. Zeus noticed the danger and destroyed Phaeton. The other is the myth of Icarus, son of Daedalus, who built wings from feathers and wax and, overwhelmed by the thrill of flying and not heeding his father's warning, flew too close to the Sun, whereupon the wax in his wings melted and he fell into the sea.

Audience: But if the Sun is our core identity, how can it take a lifetime to find it?

Clare: This is an interesting question, considering that it is Sun sign astrology which is so popular, so widely used and recognised. From a psychological point of view, the interpretation of the Sun in a birth chart is much more complex, partly because it has so many different levels of meaning and expression. I think the answer to your question is that our relationship to the Sun in our charts changes throughout our lives. It is not unusual, for example, for people to actively dislike their own Sun signs. This is a good indication that a more positive relationship can and must be forged, since the positive expression of the Sun in a chart implies a true connection to oneself and a deep level of self-acceptance. Because the Sun also describes our spiritual consciousness it is a truly awesome and powerful astrological symbol which is far too great for us to realise when we are young. It therefore tends to be projected onto, or carried by, father or male carers or father figures for the first half of our lives, until we have built a strong enough ego and are mature enough to express the full majesty of the solar principle for ourselves.

Audience: So it is essentially unconscious?

Clare: Exactly right because we are not born fully conscious. The principle of consciousness begins by being unconscious.

Audience: It may take a lifetime to realise the Sun consciously, but surely we are all living out the characteristics of our Sun signs, aren't we? Otherwise we wouldn't recognise the Sun sign descriptions so easily? For example, children seem to be very pure examples of their Sun signs, although I have noticed that they tend to lose this as they grow up. They lose that instinctive vibrancy as they learn to deal with the outside world.

Clare: Yes, as they get socialised, they stop being spontaneously themselves. As we grow up we are taught not to be selfish, to share our toys, to put others first. Once we are out of babyhood, we are taught that we are not the only special unique individuals in the world, but simply one of a group with which we are expected to conform. And so we adapt and adjust ourselves to the expectations of others. We begin the journey away from our central spiritual core and towards full involvement with the world, a journey which will, hopefully, lead us back to ourselves eventually, but this time consciously and in a more mature and integrated fashion. It is a long journey to the Sun.

My own view is that as we become socialised and develop an ego identity in order to function effectively in the world, we often take on the qualities of the sign opposite the Sun. In other words, we often manifest the polar opposite of what we really are in essence. This is worth thinking about for yourselves when we look at the meaning of the signs, but in my experience people often function as if their Sun is in the opposite sign. This seems to be a natural part of the process of development. Eventually, our fully conscious identity seems to involve the integration of our own internal opposites, both the light and the dark sides of our solar nature.

In my own work with clients, I find that it can be very helpful to focus on the conscious integration of the Sun's opposite sign and on the development of the planets which are traditionally in their detriment and fall in the Sun's sign. This helps me to see the solar principle in a wider context, as the fully integrated and mature centre of an individual's identity and indivisibility. We will look at this in more depth when we explore the expression of the Sun in each sign.

Audience: When do we become conscious?

Clare: Well, of course there are no guarantees. However, we can look at this in terms of Jung's concept of individuation. Jung believed that our lives fall naturally into two halves, with the first half involving the development of the ego, which is our sense of conscious identity, forged out of our responses to the environment into which we are born. We learn to function effectively in the world, we become socialised, develop personal skills and make relationships. During this time, various parts of our psyches remain unknown or undeveloped, as we adapt and adjust ourselves to the expectations of the outside world. The process of individuation, which is said to begin around the age of 37, involves the conscious integration of those aspects of our psyche which have, until this time, remained undeveloped and unknown to us.

Audience: So the age of 37 is the turning of the tide? Jung had a mental breakdown at that age, didn't he? He did most of his major work after that.

Clare: Yes, it was certainly the turning point in his life. We can look at this timing from an astrological point of view as well. It is not unusual for us to think we have got everything sorted by our mid-30s, but there are some extremely powerful transits which occur at the end of our 30s and beginning of our 40s which present us with what feel like completely new challenges, the experience of which are often life changing.

Audience: My father was thirty seven when he found out for the first time who his real father was.

Clare: This is a very concrete example of what we are talking about, since the Sun is the symbol of our identity, and when your father discovered his biological identity I imagine this gave him a completely new sense of himself?

Audience: Yes, he certainly changed quite radically, and took a new direction in life from that time.

MOON

The Moon's symbolism exactly opposes, complements and balances that of the Sun. The Sun is all spirit, the masculine principle, and the Moon is all soul, the feminine principle. The Sun rules the individual, and the Moon rules the collective, crowds, and groups of people generally. With no light of its own, the Moon simply reflects the light of the Sun. In this sense, the Sun is the active, or yang principle, and the Moon is the passive, or yin principle. As the Earth's satellite, the monthly cycle of the Moon is intimately connected to the tides, the growth cycle of plants and to all biological and emotional rhythms. At the full Moon emotions are heightened, we dream more, consume more alcohol, take more drugs, and even bleed more freely.

Audience: I work as a midwife and things get very interesting around the time of the full Moon! We always have higher rates of caesarean sections and bleeding and we always have an extra midwife on duty at the full Moon.

Clare: That's actually a deliberate policy?

Audience: Yes, and although I don't know of any research to support this, we have our own thesis.

Clare: I have also heard that more police are put on duty at these times, because there are more crimes, more violence and emotional explosiveness. So we can say that there are some very obvious connections between the lunar cycle and our collective emotional behaviour. This doesn't seem to be something we can control; we are caught up in it and affected by it.

Physically, the Moon rules the fluids in the body and the lymphatic system, as well as all the body's containers, such as the stomach, the womb, the bladder and the breasts. The Moon rules food, and the stomach and the breasts are connected with being fed and with feeding, the taking in and the giving out of nourishment. Looking at the list of planetary correspondences, the Moon is silver where the Sun is gold. The Moon rules watery fruits and vegetables which are round and pale, such as the cauliflower. It rules nocturnal creatures, whereas the Sun rules diurnal creatures. When it comes to people and professions, the Moon rules women generally, and anyone who is involved in the caring professions, cooks, caterers, hoteliers, housewives, midwives, nurses, as well as fishermen and other professions connected with the sea. The Moon also rules historians and genealogists because it is concerned with the past, with history, origins and ancestors. In the mundane world it rules children's homes, old people's homes, boats and ports.

Unlike the masculine, solar principle, which is single, clear and straightforward, the feminine, lunar principle is multiple, complex and changeable, like the changing phases of the Moon itself. The many triple goddess myths in our western tradition describe the lunar cycle and the three faces, or ages, of the feminine. From the three fates who spin the web of life, the three Graeae and the three Gorgons in the Perseus myth, to the three Marys in the New Testament, to the three witches in Macbeth, threeness is so embedded in the mythology of the feminine that even today people tend to react with some trepidation to the sight of three women together.

The Cast of Characters

Phases of the Moon

The triple goddess myths also reflect the phases of the Moon. The young Moon in its waxing phase is represented by the huntress Artemis or Diana, the virgin goddess of the forests, elusive, mysterious and fiercely independent, guardian of children and childbirth. The Earth goddess Demeter or Hera represents the mature, full Moon phase of woman as mother, provider and carer. This is the socially acceptable face of the feminine, fertile and nurturing. The waning, third phase of the Moon is represented by Hecate, the wise woman or crone, women past child bearing age, confident in their own feminine power and wisdom. Eventually the Moon disappears altogether into the darkest and most terrifying phase of its cycle, personified by the goddesses who rule over life and death itself, such as Lilith, destructive and vengeful, or Persephone, who holds the keys to the gates of the underworld and acts as guide to the souls of the dead.

Audience: You said there were three phases of the Moon, but there are actually four?

Clare: Yes, you are right. The fourth phase is actually the 'no Moon' phase, which is sometimes called the dark or black Moon phase, which occurs around the time of the new Moon, and describes the fearful and unacceptable face of the feminine. The black Moon phase is devouring and malevolent, ruling nightmares and black magic. It explains the collective fear of the feminine which has caused thousands of 'witches' to be drowned or burned at the stake. So you can see that the lunar symbol is full of paradox and that's as it should be because it reflects the nature of the feminine.

Psychologically the Moon rules our moods which tend to have a life of their own. They are changeable. Moods are stronger at night, we are much more suggestible, much more intuitive generally at night. Night is mysterious and fearful. Most of us will have had the experience of waking up in the middle of the night feeling fearful, overwhelmed and confused, and it is not until the solar principle returns at dawn that things become clear again and straightforward. This would be an example of experiencing the difference between the opposing but balancing lunar and solar principles.

The alchemical Moon, called Luna, from *Chymica vannus* (1666) by Joannes de Monte-Snyders. Luna in alchemical symbolism is many things, but most importantly she is the metal Mercury in female form, representing the volatile primal substance which conceals the secrets of nature.

Astrologically, the Moon rules the past, our childhood and our basic instinctual needs and habits. The Moon describes what we need in order to feel safe and nurtured and protected. The Moon in a chart describes how we experienced our mother, how we were nurtured, cared for and fed. And of course there is a very strong connection between food and mood. It is not unusual to hear someone say: "I was so angry/upset/miserable/lonely that I went to the fridge and ate everything in it." There is a strong lunar connection to eating disorders, which have to do with not having our needs fulfilled, feeling emotionally starved and vulnerable. These kinds of issues are very complex, because they operate from the instinctual depths which drive us.

A distorted Moon or lunar principle can manifest in childish demands for attention or self-destructive regressive tendencies and habits; to a clinging over-dependence, an overwhelming need to live through or for others, and to the activation of the 'psychic vampire' which leaves everyone with whom the individual comes into contact feeling drained and exhausted. Eventually, of course, every child needs to learn to feed itself, and we need to learn to feed and nurture our own Moon. Only then can we be full enough to provide emotional support for others. Although this is a very simple point, it is not uncommon for us to starve ourselves emotionally in one way or another, with the result that we become emotionally demanding, self pitying and resentful. But the Moon's placement in our birth charts indicates how we can and must learn to nurture ourselves in order restore our innate receptivity, responsiveness and sensitivity to ourselves and to others and find a loving and compassionate reconnection to our instinctual natures and to our own souls. What it is that makes us feel nurtured and safe will depend entirely on the sign in which the Moon falls, and will be very different for different people.

Audience: If you follow astrology and you know that the full Moon is going to be a particularly difficult time, is there anything you can do to prepare for it?

Clare: Working psychologically, if we sense that an impending full Moon is likely to bring our personal and emotional issues to a head, we could decide to 'go with the tide' and find a way in which the emotional heights can be experienced positively. How we do this would depend on our own personal Moon placement, but it might be appropriate to attend a dramatic and emotional opera or play or to take a day off work and visit the seaside, or go for a long walk or have a massage. Using the lunar energy in this way might mean that we can avoid a messy and distressing argument at home, or a crisis at work which suddenly seems to erupt for no reason.

Audience: Can I just ask you something which I have never understood? If your Sun is in Cancer, then that means you are ruled by the Moon, and everything about the Moon is the opposite of the Sun. I don't understand.

Clare: It is helpful to take this slowly, because the planet tells us 'what' and the sign tells us 'how'. So the Sun describes our personal identity, and because this is in the sign of Cancer, which is ruled by the Moon, we know that your personal identity will be expressed in lunar ways, perhaps by caring for others, or nurturing children, or working in a kindergarten, or cooking or running a hotel or in any area ruled by the Moon.

Audience: Yes, I can understand that. But if you have four planets in Leo and nothing else in Cancer, would you still be a lunar type because the Sun is in Cancer?

Clare: Well you would say the core centre of your being is lunar and, even though that may not become the centre of your consciousness for years and years, while you are off living the other signs because you have many planets in other signs, nevertheless at the end of the day, when you come home to yourself and to the centre of your unique personal solar identity, this will be lunar.

Audience: My Sun is at 0°04' Leo. It seems as if I am absolutely split between the two signs of Cancer and Leo.

Clare: Not really. Your Sun is in Leo. It has finished with Cancer and moved into Leo. As a matter of interest, was your birth a natural one?

Audience: I think so. I know it took a long time.

Clare: I wonder what you were waiting for?

Audience: Leo?

Clare: Yes, I think this often happens. You were waiting to be a Leo.

Audience: I'm still waiting!

MERCURY

Clare: Let's have a look at Mercury. Unlike the other planets of the old world, Mercury doesn't have an opposite or a partner because, as a symbol of paradox and contradiction, it contains all the opposites within itself. Mercury is androgynous, both male and female. It is both divisive and integrative. As the planet closest to the Sun, Mercury is the smallest and fastest, with an orbit of only 88 days. From its astronomy you can immediately see where some of our associations to Mercury come from. It darts quickly around the Sun, sometimes you see it, sometimes you don't. Sometimes it appears to be travelling in one direction, and sometimes in another. Do you have any associations with Mercury from a mythological viewpoint?

Audience: Wasn't he the messenger of the gods?

Audience: He was also a trickster and a thief. Didn't he steal some cows?

Clare: That's right. His image is that of a young boy with a winged helmet and winged sandals, holding a caduceus, a staff with two entwined serpents, often used today as a symbol for healing and medicine. Mercury is the carrier of messages and information. He has no interest in the content of the message itself; his task is simply to act as a go-between. In this sense, Mercury has no preference for right over wrong or for truth over lies. He would just as happily spread scandal and gossip as any other kind of information. He is versatile, witty, amoral, unreliable and ethereal, a kind of Puck figure from *Midsummer Night's Dream* or Ariel from *The Tempest*, or Peter Pan, who never wanted to grow up.

Audience: Amoral? You mean he has no morals?

Clare: Yes. He is perfectly happy to put the cat amongst the pigeons and stand back and watch the result. This is where Mercury's association with the rogue, the trickster, the card-sharp and the thief come from. When we describe people as 'mercurial', we mean that they are clever, certainly, but also that they are wheeler-dealers and possibly a bit dodgy.

A distorted Mercury can express itself through cunning and trickery, cheating and lying, as destructive criticism and verbal cruelty, or as a profound level of anxiety, fear and tension which erodes the immune system and undermines the body. Any of these manifestations may indicate that the archetypal gifts of Mercury – perception, intelligence, knowledge, gentle humour, genuine modesty and self confidence – have been undermined by an individual's negative experiences of the world. This would indicate a potentially fruitful area for investigation by the psychological astrologer, depending on the placement of Mercury in the chart.

Mercury rules the brain, the mind and the thinking process – it is bi-polar, ruling both left and right brain – logical thought (where something cannot be both A and not-A) and analogical thought (where something can be both A and not-A). From this point of view, Mercury rules double meanings, and double talk, double sight, double entendres, crosswords (vertical and horizontal thinking), humour and jokes. These would all be instances of seeing or hearing one thing, and then a moment later finding a deeper or different meaning to what has been

The alchemical Mercury, from *Tripus aureus* (The Golden Tripod) by Michael Maier, c. 1618. As Mercurius he presides over the alchemical opus, integrating the principles of Sun and Moon.

said. The Freudian slip is a good example of the way Mercury functions. There is a fascination with language and with words and the connections between them. So this Hermes figure is very hard to pin down, very volatile and very tricky. It is no coincidence, for example, that we say that 'my mind is playing tricks on me'. Astrologically, Mercury in the birth chart describes how each of us perceives and interprets the world, the way each of us understands, processes information, makes connections and communicates.

In common with all the other traditional planets, except for the Sun and Moon, Mercury has rulership over two signs of the zodiac, one positive and one negative, the air sign of Gemini and the earth sign of Virgo. Have a look at the various Mercury associations with Gemini and Virgo in the table of planetary correspondences. The Moon rules our babyhood, and Mercury rules our early childhood – the period when we learn to speak, we learn to walk, and we are able to explore our immediate surroundings, which will include our first relationships with our brothers and sisters. Mercury will usually describe the kind of relationship we have with our siblings – how we perceive them. Mercury's function is to carry and disseminate information.

Mercury rules the gossip which goes on in the corner shop where you buy your newspaper. In the mundane world Mercury rules schools, shops, markets, fairs, tennis. Tennis is very mercurial sport, a skilful game, passing the ball backwards and forwards. Mercury rules roads, car parks, garages, telephone exchanges, stationery, pens, pencils and books. Mercurial people love books, pens and pencils!

Audience: So Mercury is multiple.

Clare: That's right. In the animal world, it rules all small creatures of the air, such as butterflies, birds and bees, which go from plant to plant carrying pollen and cross fertilising. And small animals generally, creatures which move quickly, to-ing and fro-ing about their daily business.

Audience: So they move a lot, but not very far.

Clare: Yes, which is why Mercury rules tradesmen, postmen, couriers, people who go from house to house. Taxi drivers are another example. They take people from one place to another, but have no interest in the purpose of or reason for the journey.

Audience: So it is the sort of person who watches and facilitates but doesn't get involved themselves?

Clare: Yes, it is about making connections for its own sake, such as introducing people to each other. Secretaries, journalists and writers are mercurial people. Now we could generalise and say that journalists can be amoral, having no interest in whether what they write is true or not. The main thing is to get the story, isn't it?

Audience: My son is a Gemini and he is also a journalist. He is so like this that it is just not funny.

Clare: And I am sure he is very clever and articulate, since Gemini is a very intelligent sign.

Audience: Yes, but that doesn't help when you live with him, because you can't pin him down to anything.

Clare: Well, that's because you are not meant to.

Audience: It sounds as if Mercurial people are very child-like.

Clare: Yes, people with planets in the Mercury-ruled signs of Gemini and Virgo often look much younger than they are. This is perhaps because they are always interested in what's going on. Now that we have been discussing this planet of communication, language and making connections, I want us to start using the language of astrology as soon as we have the vocabulary. I would like you to have a look at your own charts to see if you have a contact, or aspect, in your own charts between Mercury and either your Moon or your Sun. You can see this from the grid – for the time being it doesn't matter what kind of connections, or aspects, these are since I simply want to bring together the planetary principles themselves.

Audience: I have a contact between Sun and Mercury.

Clare: This is a very common connection, because Mercury is never further than 27° from the Sun and the two planets are often connected. How would we interpret this?

Audience: That my identity is somehow connected to my ability to communicate?

Clare: Exactly right, and this is our first piece of real chart interpretation. If the Sun describes our identity then it will involve Mercury. This contact will describe the importance (Sun) or focus (Sun) on communication and information (Mercury), and is likely to be found in the charts of journalists, writers and teachers (Mercury), for example. Is this relevant in your case?

Audience: Yes, because I am a teacher. But more than that, I teach languages!

Clare: Let's look at the **Mercury-Moon** contact. This tells us that the way we think will be connected to and affected by the way we feel. This could be someone who pours a great deal of emotion into their writing, for example. It would be a good contact for a poet. On the other hand it could describe someone whose feelings muddle up their thinking, someone who finds it difficult to communicate clearly if they feel emotional about something. Moon-Mercury describes someone who is fed and nurtured by information, conversation, books, reading and/or gossip (the need to tell). Or someone whose mother (Moon) is a primary school teacher (Mercury), or perhaps a youthful mother, more like a sibling than a traditional mother figure.

It could describe a female (Moon) journalist (Mercury), or a women's (Moon) magazine (Mercury). We can play with all the words on all the different levels in the table of planetary correspondences. For example, we could have a white (Moon) car (Mercury), a woman's (Moon) bicycle (Mercury), a female (Moon) tennis player (Mercury), a silver (Moon) butterfly (Mercury), and so on. Although on one level this is just a superficial word game, it also carries much deeper astrological significance because the symbolism of these two planets is equally valid through all the levels. So, for example, it would not be surprising, except to non astrologers, to discover that a person with a Mercury-Moon contact did indeed have a white car!

Notes
1. "Archetypes appear in the form of mythological, symbolic representations which are common to whole peoples or epochs" C.G. Jung, *Psychological Types*, para 747.
2. Howard Sasportas, 'Subpersonalities and Psychological Conflicts' in Liz Greene and Howard Sasportas: *The Development of the Personality: Seminars in Psychological Astrology, Volume 1*.
3. Pierro Ferrucci, *What We May Be*.

LESSON 3

Venus and Mars

Our next pair of planets, which are both complementary and opposite astrological principles, are Venus and Mars. Mythically they are either lovers or bitter enemies, often both at the same time. Jung described the complexity of this in his description of the alchemical mystical marriage between male and female: '… we are inclined to think of this primarily as the power of love, of passion, which drives the two opposite poles together, forgetting that such a vehement attraction is needed only when an equally strong resistance keeps them apart'.[1] From a psychological point of view, these two planets need each other, because they keep each other in balance and harmony. Venus without Mars, and Mars without Venus are very sorry creatures indeed, and without each other these two planetary principles are very likely to become distorted with the result that everything starts to go wrong.

These two planets become particularly important around the time of adolescence, when we start to explore our own individuality as a way of growing away from, or defining ourselves against, the parental Sun/Moon matrix. Venus and Mars concern the feminine and masculine aspects of desire and sexuality, the extraordinarily powerful forces which arrive with adolescence and which are often quite overwhelming until we can find a relatively stable relationship with them. Venus and Mars are extremely powerful forces in every one of us, with Venus representing the force of attraction and Mars representing the force of assertion. One way to illustrate this is to think of Venus as 'egg consciousness' and Mars as 'sperm consciousness'. Venus seeks to attract and, in fact, chooses. Mars seeks to compete and to win.

A distorted Venus which has become bitter, vicious, jealous and possessive, or greedy, inert, vain and selfish, needs attention. The pure archetypal qualities of Venus, of love, fulfilment and joy, have become lost. A distorted Mars which has become violent, destructive, aggressive and reckless or weak and self sacrificial also needs attention. The pure archetypal qualities of Mars, the gift of strength and potency, have been lost. It is developmentally crucial that the full creative potential of Venus and Mars are explored and developed, since it is these two planets which affirm life and which are the seat of our personal sense of joy, fulfilment, strength and potency, qualities which enable us to live our lives with passion and enthusiasm.

The placement of Venus and Mars in our birth charts will indicate how and where we need to develop these qualities to their full potential. As with the Sun and Moon, the principles of Venus and Mars are not gender related, since both planets are found in every chart. What is important, therefore, is for each individual to explore and understand and to honour what their Venus desires and how their Mars needs to assert itself.

VENUS

As one of the two 'feminine' planets, the first point to make about Venus is that she is not the Moon. The Moon describes our deep emotional attachments and needs, whereas Venus is potentially a much more conscious principle which affirms the individual and describes our tastes and values and talents as well as our own individual appreciation of what is beautiful and valuable. Where Venus is concerned, beauty is definitely in the eye of the beholder.

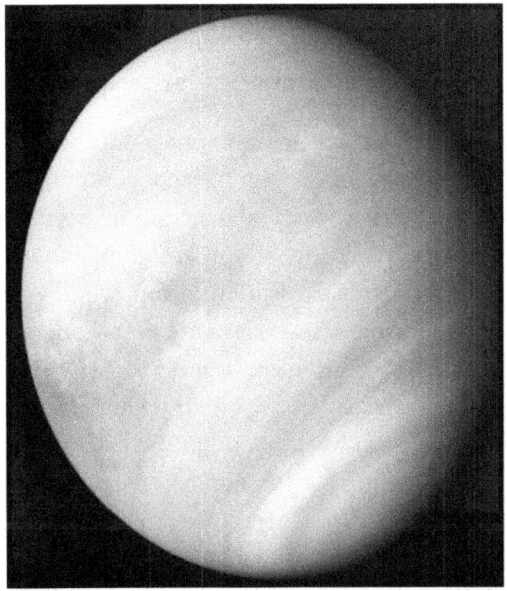

An image of Venus from an alchemical text by Nicola d'Antonio degli Agli (1480), portraying her as the volatile female element in the alchemical opus. The emblem on her throne represents her metal, copper. Taurus and Libra, the zodiac signs she rules, are shown below.

Venus is the power of attraction or, to put it another way, she is 'pulling power', which is a very powerful force indeed. Imagine that you are walking down a street and you see something in a shop window that attracts you. Before you realise what you are doing, you will find yourself walking towards it, because it is pulling you, whether it is a piece of jewellery, or a car part, or the latest computer, or a work of art. It attracts you, and there is a kind of fascination or mesmerising power. This is the power of Venus – she 'turns us on'. A similar thing happens when we are watching somebody in a film who we find particularly attractive. Attraction is not confined to things or to people: we can be attracted just as powerfully to aesthetic values and principles, to brilliant minds, to ideals of justice and fairness, to qualities of courage and honour, to music, art and dance.

Venus describes what gives us joy, regardless of the opinions of others. Whether or not our culture sanctions our particular individual pleasures, Venus needs to be fulfilled if we are to find joy in our lives. This is not as easy as it sounds because the Venus principle has become so collectively mistrusted, judged and distorted that we don't have to delve very far into our religious or cultural backgrounds before we find that 'woman' (Venus) is self-indulgent, selfish, lustful, greedy, dangerous, devouring, seductive, desireful and, not uncommonly, plain evil. The Venus principle seems to have become socially and culturally acceptable only to the extent that it has been channelled into the accumulation of wealth and possessions which, when achieved, often prove to have been distractions, empty substitutes for the true joy and pleasure we were seeking. So Venus needs to be redeemed both culturally and on a personal level. In my experience, there is almost always important work to be done according to the placement of Venus in our birth charts. It is almost the norm that we will be denying ourselves the full creative expression of Venus in our charts.

Venus has rulership over two zodiac signs, one positive and active and one negative and passive, which can be associated to Venus as the morning star and as the evening star. Venus rules the negative earth sign of Taurus and the positive air sign of Libra. So Venus rules both the earthy, sensual, gentle sign of Taurus and the aesthetic, civilised, principled values of the sign of Libra.

You will see from the table of planetary correspondences that Venus rules fruit and flowers, both symbols of the feminine. Beauty, wealth, comfort, jewellery, cosmetics are all ruled by Venus, as are the colours of nature, pale blues and pinks. As ruler of Libra, Venus is associated with all the civilised arts, with justice, diplomacy, equality, compatibility. Her metal is copper, which is a beautiful soft, glowing metal. In the body, Venus rules the neck and the throat, and the voice can be a very sensuous medium, can't it? Taureans often have beautiful voices and can be wonderful singers. As ruler of Libra, Venus rules the kidneys, whose function is to keep the body in balance and in harmony with itself.

Audience: My mother is always saying that if you don't respect your Venus you are risking your voice and your kidneys.

Clare: Yes, because if we deny any one of the planets its full positive expression, it will tend to get its own back on a physical plane.

Where do you find Venusian people? They can be artists and musicians, of course, or jewellers, models, bankers, since money is such a symbol of worth, diplomats, receptionists, beauticians, farmers. In the mundane world Venus rules gardens, wardrobes, dressing tables, cosmetics, art galleries and concert halls. Everything and anything which makes life more harmonious, peaceful and beautiful. As the planet which describes our taste and values and talents, what is of worth to us, even what makes life worth living, Venus needs to be indulged. Now if we deny ourselves the positive expression of Venus in our charts, Venus doesn't go away, she gets angry. Every personal planet needs to be fully acknowledged and encouraged. If Venus gets what she wants, she will be satisfied and fulfilled. If she is denied what she wants, she will become voracious, vicious and demanding, with often devastating results.

We will look at the various different desires of Venus when we come to look at the expression of Venus in the zodiac signs. This can be a really enjoyable astrological exercise, to find out what we really enjoy and give ourselves permission to have a bit more of it in our lives. We can also look to the Venus placement of our friends, families and partners for ideas about what presents they will enjoy, value and appreciate. This is very well worth doing and a lovely example of astrology in practice. Venus in the chart will also describe how and where we are talented, where we have the gift of the goddess. Naturally, we tend not to value our talents, thinking that 'everyone can do this', which is not true because it points to our own particular unique talents and capacity for joyful creativeness.

Audience: So what we are attracted to will be shown by the sign that our Venus is in?

Clare: Yes, and according to the house it falls in as well as to the aspects it makes. At the moment we are taking it all apart and looking at the individual pieces of the jigsaw. The planets describe principles, which need to be looked at in isolation, or in relation to each other, before we combine them with other factors. When we start to include the other factors, such as the signs, houses and the meaning of the planetary aspects themselves, the picture will be increasingly refined and we will gain a much deeper and more accurate understanding of each individual's chart.

Planetary Pairs
Have a look at our example charts, and you will see that Sally has a **Sun-Venus** contact. This describes her perception of her father (Sun) as a gentle and loving (Venus) man, whose praise and appreciation (Venus) would have been of value to her (Venus). This is likely to be extended to her partners in later life and she is likely to value (Venus) people with attractive and pleasant natures (Venus). With Venus connected to her sense of identity (Sun), she may become a musician or a gardener, lawyer, architect or beautician (Venus).

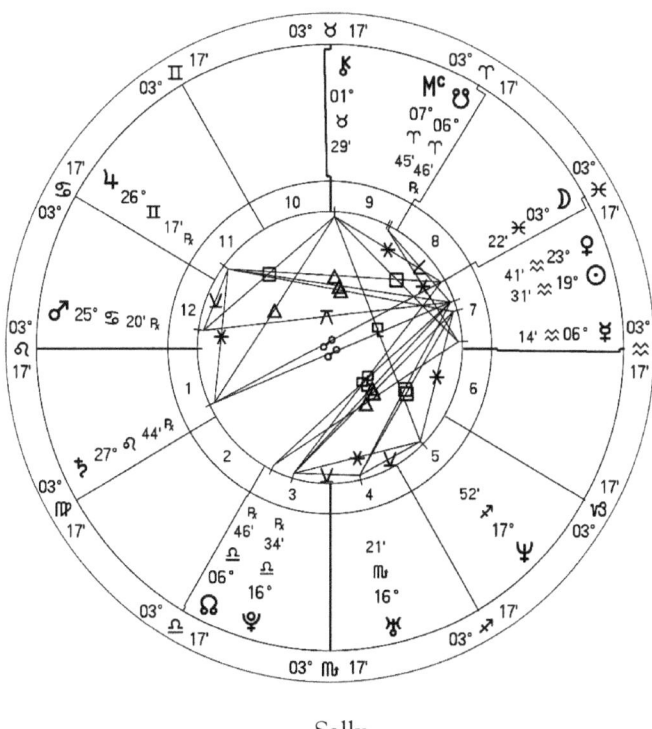

Sally

David, on the other hand, has a **Moon-Venus** contact in his chart. This indicates that he valued and loved (Venus) his mother (Moon), and this is likely to extend to valuing and appreciating women (Venus) generally. He needs (Moon) peace and tranquillity (Venus) and will have a gentle, sensitive and caring nature.

Mercury-Venus would describe someone who has a love (Venus) of words (Mercury), who could be a writer or an actor or even a collector of valuable books. They may have a gift (Venus) with words (Mercury) and are likely to be diplomatic and charming (Venus) in conversation (Mercury).

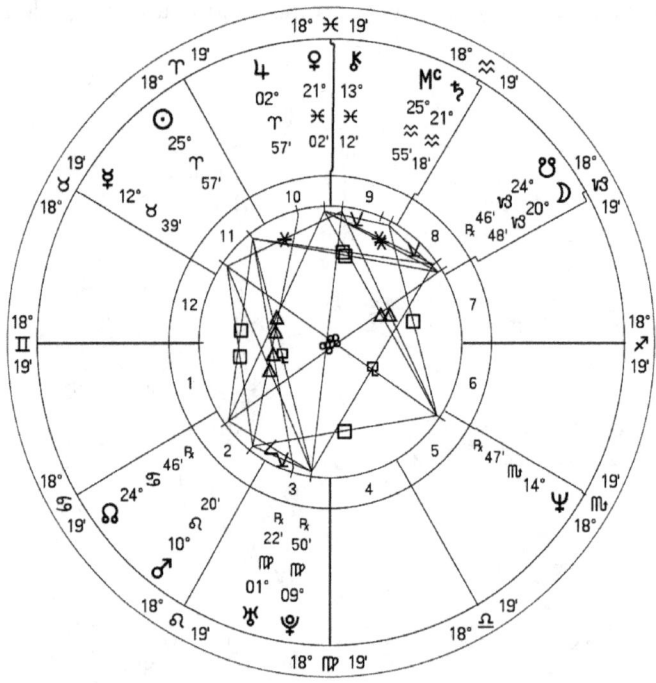

David

MARS

Mars is the first of the 'superior' planets, lying outside the orbit of the Earth, with an orbit of approximately two years. As the red planet, it has always been associated with passion and anger, with its two satellites Phobos and Daimos meaning fear and terror. Astrologically, if Venus tells us what we value and what we desire, Mars describes how we go about getting it. Venus and Mars need to work together. Mars is the principle of assertion and outward directed action, describing our personal drive and how we assert ourselves. We all need a good enough defence system, don't we, in order to protect ourselves if necessary and to act when action is needed. Without this, we can be easily manipulated, undermined and taken advantage of. Although we all have very different ways of reaching our goals, Mars is fundamentally competitive, concerned with the will to live and to survive.

Mars is a very physical planet, ruling adrenalin, the iron in the blood, the muscles, the genitals and the body's excretory system. So it describes the particular qualities of our physical, emotional and mental strength, which need to be harnessed to our will to survive. You will see from the

The alchemical Mars slays the primordial dragon in order to release the tincture which leads to the alchemical gold. The image is from *De lapide philosophico* (1625) by the German philosopher Lambsprinck.

table of planetary correspondences that Mars rules furnaces, barracks, weapons, knives, slaughterhouses, blood, inflammation, muscles, the sexual drive, fevers, soldiers, bloodshed, sportsmen, firemen, iron, surgeons, dentists, the martial arts, stinging and thorn-bearing plants (nettles), radishes, hot food and spices. In the birth chart, Mars describes how we stand up for, assert and defend ourselves. It is where we 'see red', how we express our personal drive, our anger and our passion, our sexuality.

As the ruler of the active fire sign of Aries, Mars is instinctive and spontaneous, hot-headed and aggressive. Mars can be extremely rash and brutal, and once the 'blood is up' Mars can succumb to the 'blood lust' which leads to rape, pillage and general carnage. Mars can be found 'spoiling for a fight' on the football terraces, in pub fights fuelled by alcohol, in gang rapes, violent murders and in 'road rage'. It can be very frightening to witness this kind of brutal rage, where the people involved have lost their humanity and there is no reasoning with them until the adrenalin eventually subsides. This would be an example of Mars functioning on its own without any sign of Venus. On the other hand, with the support of Venus, this very same energy can be harnessed to compete, achieve and win against impossible odds, and we often admire and are inspired by heroic stories about people surviving, winning and achieving in spite of impossible odds.

As ruler of the passive water sign of Scorpio, Mars is more subtle and controlled. This Mars is also a fighter, but highly trained and disciplined in the controlled use of energy and aggression, an efficient killing machine whose strength and courage is dedicated not to personal survival but to the survival of the whole, or to a greater cause.

Audience: This reminds me of the film *Gladiator*. The hero was actually a very gentle man, a natural and courageous leader who inspired the loyalty of his troops and who dedicated himself and his life to the defence of the ideal of the Roman republic.

Clare: Yes, this is an excellent example. In this sense, the hero was a 'sacred warrior' dedicating his life and his skills to the survival of something greater than himself. His Venus is involved because he is fighting for what he values. The Scorpio expression of Mars uses the knife in a very skilled and disciplined way. This could be a surgeon or a dentist, for example, anyone who uses knives and other sharp instruments with great precision in the service of healing others. The controlled use of physical energy and aggression is also essential for sportsmen and athletes.

So, you can see that Mars can be immensely effective or immensely destructive. Perhaps the most important thing to say about Mars is that it is essential that its energy is expressed outwards if we are to feel confident and capable in the world. If the energy of Mars is blocked, it doesn't simply go away but turns back on the individual, back onto ourselves, which means that we will attract and invite violence into our lives from the outside world. Masochism is an example of turning the Mars energy against ourselves. This blocked energy can also have serious physical effects, resulting in various illnesses or in depressions which are caused by the suppression of anger. We must find an outer channel for this energy.

Audience: Do you have a connection between Mars and Venus if there is no aspect between them?

Clare: Well, even if they are not in aspect, provided each has what it wants, with Venus being properly fulfilled and Mars being properly used up, they can still support each other. All we have to do is find out what they want and make sure they have enough of it, because so much of our personal sense of fulfilment and joy and potency depends on these two planets, which affirm and strengthen and support our individual development. As psychological astrologers, I think one of our most important tasks is to explore the seven traditional planets in depth, discover how they are functioning in an individual's life, and work to redeem and release their archetypal and individual potential. Obviously, 'the process of psychological differentiation is no light work',[2] but these planets, functioning well, enable us to build a healthy sense of personal identity and an ego structure strong enough to protect us from being overwhelmed by the powerful collective forces represented by the outer planets and by Chiron.

Planetary Pairs

As you can see, David has a **Mars-Mercury** contact. This means that he will, or should, develop the ability to assert himself and defend himself (Mars) with words (Mercury). He is likely to have a sharp (Mars) mind (Mercury) and speak (Mercury) to the point (Mars). Sibling (Mercury) rivalry (Mars) is likely to have been his training ground. He may even find himself in a profession, such as the law, where he fights (Mars) with words (Mercury). It is possible that he has ongoing arguments (Mars) with his neighbours (Mercury) and that he drives a sports (Mars) car (Mercury). Can you get a sense of David coming alive as a real person with these descriptions?

Sally, on the other hand, has a **Mars-Venus** contact. She is likely to get her own way (Mars) by being charming or seductive (Venus). She could be very attracted to (Venus) qualities of strength, determination and power (Mars) in herself and in others. She is likely to love (Venus) competition (Mars) and be skilled in the art (Venus) of war (Mars).

Audience: I have a Mars-Moon contact. How does that work?

Clare: Well, this would indicate your need (Moon) for autonomy and independence (Mars). It could describe your mother (Moon) as a strong or competitive (Mars) woman, against whom you will define your own independence (Mars). This can be a tremendously protective combination, the female animal who will fight to the death (Mars) to protect her young (Moon), and from whom predators will normally, and quite rightly, steer clear. There is a female warrior quality to this combination, the tribe of the Amazons would be a good example, but with the fluctuating energy levels of the Moon, this emotional (Moon) aggression (Mars) is likely to be tidal (Moon), with periods of exhaustion following periods of aggression and assertion. This could also describe someone with a tendency to stomach (Moon) ulcers (Mars).

Audience: Funny you should say this, because I have been fighting my mother since I was born!

Notes
1. C. G. Jung, *Mysterium Coniunctionis*, p.89.
2. C. G. Jung, *The Psychology of the Transference*, p.132.

LESSON 4

Jupiter and Saturn

Jupiter and Saturn form another pair of opposites which can be broadly defined as the principles of expansion and contraction, faith and fear, enthusiasm and inhibition. When these two planets are supporting each other, Saturn will provide structure and shape to the vision and faith of Jupiter. Without Saturn, Jupiter would remain ungrounded and unrealistic, unable to manifest itself in the world. Without Jupiter, there would be no purpose or meaning to the structures created by Saturn. Jupiter is the entrepreneur with the vision, and Saturn is the ability to turn the vision into reality. We need both.

As social planets Jupiter and Saturn describe our experiences of the outside world and what we therefore expect from the world. From a developmental point of view, Jupiter and Saturn begin to come into their own as we stand on the threshold of adulthood. When the time comes for us to engage with the world as adults, to find work and to support ourselves emotionally and financially, we discover that, according to the nature of Jupiter and Saturn in our charts, our assumptions about how easy or difficult this will be, will be confirmed by the world's response.

Audience: So are you saying that, where these two planets are involved, we get what we expect?

Clare: Yes, and this is a very important point. For example, as the principle of faith, enthusiasm and expansion, the world will often 'oblige' by giving us a charmed path according to the Jupiter position in our charts. As the principle of fear and inhibition, Saturn is equally pleased to oblige us by providing the obstacles and difficulties we anticipate, therefore reinforcing our expectations of the world.

Audience: Does this mean that if we change our expectations then the world's response will also change?

Clare: The short answer to this question is yes, but of course it is not as simple as it sounds because there is a natural balancing mechanism in the psyche between the principles of Jupiter and Saturn, which points to the fact that they need to be equally acknowledged and developed. According to the law of opposites, every polarity, pushed to its extreme, will become its opposite. For example, if we push our luck where Jupiter is concerned we will eventually become excessively arrogant, overbearing, complacent and careless. This will evoke Saturn, and we will find ourselves alone to the extent that we are excluded, restricted or rejected. On the other hand, if we give Saturn his due, take nothing for granted, take the long hard road, suffer isolation, pessimism and periods of depression, eventually we may find, if we are fortunate, that a deep 'hard won' faith gradually emerges which, built on the hard rock of experience, nobody can take away from us. We will have found Jupiter. Clearly, neither extreme is advisable! We need to develop a positive relationship to both these planets in our birth charts, so that neither one becomes too extreme and each supports the other.

As social planets, Jupiter rules the benevolent face of society and Saturn rules the restrictive face of society. Jupiter rules our civic rights and all the amenities provided by the government or by society for the benefit of civilians; employment protection and equal opportunities laws, child and unemployment benefits, legal aid, hospitals, refuse collection, sports centres, concert halls, libraries, schools and universities. In this sense, Jupiter rules the 'they' whose job it is to provide all these services. As children, or for as long as we remain psychologically infantile, we expect 'them' to be the benevolent parents who provide for all our needs without us having to do anything.

Saturn rules the stern face of society and all the laws and amenities which are put in place for the safety and necessary containment of civilians: the police force and armed services, prisons and detention centres, rules and regulations, law courts, fines, penalties, punishments, imprisonment. As children, or for as long as we remain psychologically infantile, we tend to experience 'them' as restricting critical parents against whom we can rail against but who wield power over us as long as we remain under their control.

Ultimately, the principles of Jupiter and Saturn need to be owned and integrated within our own psyches if we are to become psychologically adult. This means that we need to find our own Jupiter, our own god or gods, beliefs and principles which give our lives meaning, and these may in fact be quite different from the culture in which we live. And we need to find our own Saturn, our own inner authority and our own personal laws by which we live. If we can develop these two principles in such a way that they are no longer projected or carried by society for us, then we can make a positive and useful and valuable contribution to the society in which we live.

JUPITER

Jupiter is the largest planet in the solar system, ten times the size of the Earth. With its permanent storms, great red spot, axial rotation of approximately ten hours and its family of moons, everything about Jupiter is larger than life, active, turbulent, stormy and grand. In Greek mythology, Jupiter/Zeus was king of the gods and ruler of Mount Olympus. As the youngest and most fortunate of all his brothers and sisters, who were swallowed at birth by their father Saturn/Chronos, Jupiter was protected in his youth, leading a charmed existence. When he grew up he became his father's cup bearer and gave him a brew which caused Saturn/Chronos to vomit up all his previously swallowed brothers and sisters. From this moment on, Saturn was banished to the outermost reaches of the solar system and Jupiter became king of the gods, ruling on Mount Olympus.

In the horoscope, Jupiter expands whatever it touches. Jupiter describes what we believe in, what we have faith in, where we are

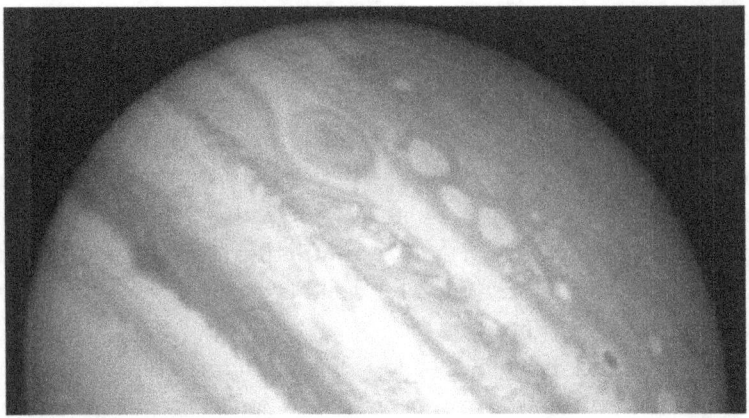

An image of Jupiter releasing his eagles into the world, from *Atalanta fugiens* (1618), an alchemical text by Michael Maier.

optimistic, confident and expect things to go well for us. Jupiter is our personal cornucopia, the horn of plenty which never runs dry. It is playful, restless, fertile, easily bored, always seeking new adventures and wider horizons. Jupiter is imaginative and creative and likes to do things in a big way. It lends conviction. As the planet of faith, Jupiter describes our belief system, our philosophy and our sense of what makes life worth living, indicating where we seek to grow, to expand and find meaning in our lives. Jupiter describes our sense of abundance and our spiritual wellbeing. Like a balloon, Jupiter tends to go on expanding until it bursts dramatically. However often it crashes and burns, there is normally enough faith to begin again and repeat the expansion all over again.

Jupiter gives us a feeling of omnipotence, and describes how and where we 'play god', riding roughshod over other people's feelings and sensitivities. There can be a remarkable hubris and arrogance where Jupiter is in the chart. It describes where and how we are likely to become inflated and where we can be boastful, patronising and condescending. Jupiter can't bear limitation and as such can describe where we are discontented and greedy, always wanting more. An inflated or fanatical Jupiter reveals a distortion of the archetypal quality of this planet. At root, Jupiter is the gift of enthusiasm and faith.

Planetary Pairs
David has a **Jupiter-Mars** connection. How would you interpret this?

Audience: Could he have a philosophy or belief in war?

Clare: Absolutely. He may be very interested, for example, in war games. He may be one of those people who dresses up in uniform and re-enacts the scenes of historical battles. At any rate, he is likely to be someone who fights (Mars) for a cause (Jupiter), a crusader. He will have a strong belief (Jupiter) in strength and potency (Mars). There is something larger than life (Jupiter) about his need to assert and defend himself (Mars).

Sally has an interesting combination of planets connected to Jupiter – Sun, Moon, Venus and Mars. Let's look at these separately. The **Jupiter-Sun** aspect tells us something about Sally's innate personal (Sun) faith and optimism (Jupiter). There will be something larger than life (Jupiter) about her, and she is likely to be generous and gregarious (Jupiter). She will have experienced her father (Sun) as a larger than life character, exciting and adventurous, perhaps even godlike (Jupiter). Depending on the other chart factors, she may even have found him overwhelming (Jupiter). She is generous, buoyant, enthusiastic, and possibly arrogant, unrealistic and over-optimistic.

The **Jupiter-Moon** combination describes Sally's expansive and exaggerated (Jupiter) feelings (Moon). She can easily find herself on an emotional (Moon) rollercoaster (Jupiter) as her feelings expand and contract (Moon) dramatically (Jupiter). She will be instinctively (Moon) optimistic (Jupiter), and needs (Moon) plenty of freedom, adventure and opportunity (Jupiter). Her mother (Moon) is likely to be generous, optimistic or philosophical (Jupiter), someone who taught her that life is an adventure to be explored whenever possible (Jupiter).

Jupiter-Venus indicates that Sally will have a love (Venus) of travel (Jupiter) and an appreciation (Venus) of other cultures and religions (Jupiter). She has a great capacity (Jupiter) for enjoyment (Venus), and is likely to be attracted to (Venus) people who can help her develop her knowledge and experience (Jupiter) and to any new adventures (Jupiter).

As with David's chart, the **Jupiter-Mars** combination indicates that Sally is likely to have enormous (Jupiter) physical energy (Mars) and will believe in (Jupiter) fighting for a cause (Mars).

Now that we have looked at each of these Jupiter connections, are you getting a sense of Sally's personality?

Audience: Yes, she certainly seems larger than life. I am not sure I like her, though. Too over the top for me.

Audience: This is a tremendously enthusiastic person. I expect she is very generous and loving. The sort of person who would leap in to rescue you if you needed her. But could you trust her at the end of the day?

Clare: Well, it is perfectly possible that the next time you phoned her you would probably find she had left the country on another adventure.

SATURN

Saturn is the second largest planet in the solar system, after Jupiter. Visually, it is the most beautiful of all the planets, clearly defined and cold, with its most obvious characteristic being the rings which surround it. It has its own boundaries. Mythologically, Saturn/Chronos ruled the old world, which is often referred to as the golden age. Saturn swallowed his children as soon as they were born, because an oracle had predicted that he would be overthrown by one of them. He was fearful of losing his authority, his control and his power. Eventually, of course, he was indeed overthrown by his son Jupiter and banished to the outermost boundary of the solar system.

Saturn is the planet of darkness, cold and death. It is the principle of restriction and limitation in time and space. In this sense, Saturn is the reality principle, since none of us can escape the fact that we are physically mortal and restricted and defined by the actual circumstances

of our lives. As lord of time, Saturn rules our allotted life spans, cutting the thread of life with his sickle when the appointed time comes. Unlike Jupiter, there is no 'getting away with it' where Saturn is concerned. As the god of agriculture, Saturn describes the idea that 'as we sow, so shall we reap'. Where Saturn is involved, unless we plan in advance and make the necessary preparations and do the necessary work, and have the patience to wait, we will not achieve our goals. Wisdom comes as the result of age, experience and the recognition of realistic limitations.

Saturn is the threshold, the boundary and the ego structure without which we are unable to function effectively in the world. Saturn is also known as the great teacher, describing the hard work and the difficult lessons we need to master our lives, regardless of the obstacles which appear to obstruct us. It represents parental and authority figures, whoever it is who defines the 'oughts, shoulds and musts' in our lives. If we can learn Saturn's lessons, however, then we will gain our own sense of personal authority and responsibility which nobody can take away from us. From an alchemical point of view, Saturn is the lead without which it would be impossible to make gold.

A Saturn which is functioning in a cynical, critical and rigid fashion is a distortion of the archetype of practical wisdom. Ultimately, Saturn is the gift of self sufficiency. In the birth chart, Saturn describes what we crave but feel we have been denied. It is where we feel awkward and deficient, as if we cannot do anything right. Saturn describes what we take seriously, and where we have a marked lack of humour and spontaneity. We are often highly defended and defensive where Saturn is, because this is where we are particularly sensitive to criticism and afraid of being humiliated. Although Saturn's boundaries can protect us, taken to extremes they can become rigid, constricting and suffocating. If Jupiter describes how and where we feel confident, Saturn describes how and where we feel fearful and vulnerable and where we experience limitation, frustration and a lack of confidence. Saturn indicates the hard lessons we need to learn, where we will not get anything unless we pay our dues. Saturn consolidates and concentrates, strips everything down to the bare bones, indicating where we have to become realistic, where we eventually learn to accept our limitations.

An image from Michael Maier's alchemical text, *Atalanta fugiens* (1618), showing Saturn (the prima materia or raw substance) being transformed through the calcinatio, the process of burning away dross and black bile.

Let's put Saturn together with some of the other planets to see how it functions in aspect. The **Saturn-Moon** contact can describe someone who is emotionally (Moon) inhibited (Saturn), or emotionally (Moon) starved (Saturn), or who has a fear (Saturn) of being unsafe (Moon). A fear (Saturn) of being needy (Moon) can lead to emotional (Moon) self-sufficiency (Saturn). The Saturn-Moon person may take responsibility (Saturn) for the care (Moon) of others, or this placement could indicate a working (Saturn), older (Saturn) mother (Moon). There is usually a strong need (Moon) for safety and security (Saturn).

Someone with a **Saturn-Venus** contact may be cautious or inhibited (Saturn) in relationships (Venus), possibly as the result of a lack (Saturn) of self worth (Venus). On the other hand they can show great commitment (Saturn) in relationships (Venus). They are likely to value themselves (Venus) according to their achievements in the world (Saturn), and find it difficult (Saturn) to relax (Venus). They will desire (Venus) to prove themselves to others (Saturn). Pleasures (Venus) will be taken seriously (Saturn), and this is an individual who may value (Venus) social status (Saturn) or old things which have stood the test of time (Saturn).

Both Sally and David have Moon-Saturn and Venus-Saturn contacts in their charts. We have already seen that David has a gentle Moon-Venus contact. Now that Saturn is added to the picture we can understand that he is likely to be cautious about making commitments, and will wait for some time before he feels he can trust. In Sally's case, on the other hand, we have already seen that her Jupiter-Sun-Moon-Venus-Mars contacts could be fairly overwhelming, over the top and unrealistic. Adding Saturn to the picture is likely to provide an element of stability and caution which will enable her to structure her natural enthusiasm and ground her vision, turning it into something useful and effective.

The Old World

For so long as Saturn remained the boundary of the solar system, the Sun, Moon and five planets explained and defined the totality of human experience in a remarkably complete and comprehensive way. Symbolically, the number seven is a number of completion, harmony and balance. There are seven notes in the octave, seven colours in the rainbow, seven wonders of the world and seven 'ages of man', describing our expanding awareness as we grow to maturity:

> All the world's a stage, and all the men and women merely players: they have their exits and their entrances; and one man in his time plays many parts, his acts being seven ages.[1]

The Planetary Days

The seven days of the week are particularly significant astrologically, since each of the days in the week is named after one of the planets. This table describes the derivation of the names of the days of the week:

Day	Planet	Derivation
Sunday	Sun's Day	French: Dimanche German: Sonntag (Sun's day) Italian: Domenica (Lord's day)
Monday	Moon's Day	French: Lundi (la Lune) German: Montag (Moon's day) Italian: Lunedi
Tuesday	Mars' Day	French: Mardi German: Dienstag Italian: Martedi Anglo-Saxon: Tiwesdaeg, after the Teutonic god of war
Wednesday	Mercury's Day	French: Mercredi German: Mittwoch ('midweek'), but associated with Wotan or Wodin (Odin), a shape-shifter god of wisdom, poetry and magic words, lord of the runes Italian: Mercoledi
Thursday	Jupiter's Day	French: Jeudi, derived from the Roman god Jove German: Donnerstag, 'thunder day', after Thor, the Norse god of thunder Italian: Giovedi (Jove's day)
Friday	Venus' Day	French: Vendredi German: Freitag Italian: Venerdi Anglo-Saxon: Frigedaeg, the goddess Freya's day
Saturday	Saturn's Day	French: Samedi German: Samstag Italian: Sabato (Sabbath) Anglo-Saxon: Saeternesdaeg

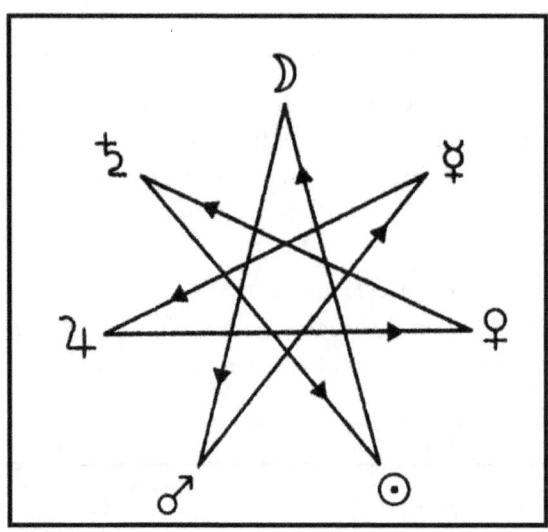

What is interesting about the seven pointed star above is that, if you follow the arrows from planet to planet, they describe the order of the days of the week. In addition to this, the planets around the outside of the star follow the ancient 'Chaldean' order of the planets, based on their increasing speed from the point of view of the Earth: Saturn, Jupiter, Mars, Sun, Venus, Mercury, Moon. You may even remember the traditional nursery rhyme describing the characteristics of people born on each day of the week:

> **Monday's** child is fair of face (round and pale like the Moon)
> **Tuesday's** child is full of grace (the strength and grace of an athlete
>   – Mars)
> **Wednesday's** child is full of woe (after the Wotan or Wode,
>   inventor of language and writing, compared to Mercury)
> **Thursday's** child has far to go (after the wide ranging and restless
>   god Thor – Scandinavian god of thunder)
> **Friday's** child is loving and giving (with the qualities of Venus)
> **Saturday's** child works hard for a living (with the qualities of Saturn)
> But the child who is born on the Sabbath day (**Sunday**) is bonny
>   and blithe and good and gay (with the qualities of the Sun)

The point about this is that for thousands of years astrology has been based on the idea of seven as the number of completion. Saturn represented the ultimate temporal authority, the 'ring pass not' of the solar system and of the psyche. The discovery of the three outer planets and of Chiron has catapulted us into a very new world indeed, and we will look at these next.

Notes
1. William Shakespeare, *As You Like It*, Act II, Scene 7.

LESSON 5

The Outer Planets

Clare: I want to look at the outer planets this evening. We need to approach them with caution, since they are of an altogether different order to the seven traditional planets and it is important that, as astrologers, we always keep this in mind. If Saturn describes our ego boundary, then these planets lie outside the orbit, or control, of the ego. What's your understanding of the ego? How would you define it?

Audience: The individual.

Clare: Yes, the ego can be described as the adapted part of ourselves with which we are identified, the part of ourselves which has learned how to function in the world. We are not born with an ego structure, it is something we develop. It gives us a sense of identity, personal control and relative autonomy, represented by the planet Saturn. Saturn is about being contained within a safe boundary, and a good strong ego structure keeps us safe. The outer planets are beyond the control of our ego and each, in its own way, threatens our ego boundaries and our sense of being in control.

Audience: Are you saying that, no matter what we do, the outer planets are beyond our control, no matter how hard we try? That we can control the planets out to Saturn, but not the outer planets?

Clare: Yes, we can certainly try to control them, and often do, but it is not going to work because they are, by their nature, outside our personal control. For instance, we can all get to know and learn how to use our own Mars so that it serves us and, in that sense, it is brought under the control of the ego. Equally, once we understand the function of Jupiter in our own charts, what we have faith in and what gives us a sense of meaning, this can be harnessed and developed under our ego control. When it comes to the outer planets and to Chiron, however, we need to find a way not of controlling, but of negotiating with them if they are to function positively in our lives. I hope this will become clearer as we develop these ideas further.

Uranus, Neptune and Pluto have always existed in the solar system, but their sequential discoveries in 1781, 1846 and 1930 reflect an extraordinary expansion of human awareness and a growing realisation that there are collective forces at work which subsume our small contained worlds of individual, family, community, society and country. Of course, this is nothing new, because unexpected and unexplained events and phenomena have always existed but, for so long as Saturn formed the boundary of the old world, the principles now associated with these three planets were projected onto supernatural forces, both divine and diabolic, originating entirely beyond the human sphere. From an astrological perspective, however, whatever is discovered 'out there' in the solar system is also ready to be discovered 'in here' within each human psyche. The discovery of the outer planets has dramatically expanded our collective awareness and our collective responsibilities, in ways which I think we are still struggling to understand and integrate. Nick Campion writes:

> Perhaps in the Age of Aquarius we will recognise the presence of the Divine within us, rather than projecting it outward onto various superhuman gods and goddesses. Human beings will have to acknowledge themselves as the source of both good and evil, and of all the other possibilities on earth. Change depends upon individual free will, and the development of the individual capacity to make independent choices. The 'new age' will therefore come about not as a result of a preordained pattern but as a result of the ability of humanity to realise its full potential.[1]

One of the first clues to their astrological interpretation is the fact that the metals Uranium, Neptunium and Plutonium, which were named after the three outer planets, are all highly toxic, poisonous, radioactive and naturally unstable. With the development of sub-atomic physics, their immense power and energy has already been harnessed in ways which profoundly affect us all. Now that this Pandora's box has been opened we are faced with the increasingly urgent question of how to integrate these principles positively on a psychological level. If we identify with these collective forces, they have a habit of overwhelming our personal ego boundaries and functioning as autonomous forces. This can be immensely powerful and creative, to the extent that our lives are consciously devoted to serving the collective but, as Jung often pointed out, we need a strong enough ego structure to be able to contain this process. Does this make any sense to you?

Audience: But if we believe in the growth and evolution of consciousness, then surely they have very positive functions as well?

Clare: Yes, they also represent immensely positive developments which appear to describe a genuine evolution of consciousness. The secret seems to be for each of us to find the right relationship to the outer planets. If we allow ourselves to become passive victims, or alternatively try to harness their influence for our own personal gain, then we are likely to become inflated and start to believe that we are omniscient (Uranus), omnipresent (Neptune) or omnipotent (Pluto) and that is too big for us, insofar as we are ordinary mortals. It is no coincidence that these three planets also rule mental breakdowns, insanity, self delusion, messiah complexes, in addition to suffering and megalomania. We need an ego structure which is strong enough to 'suffer the gods', as Jung so beautifully expressed it. As you can see, I am on a mission when it comes to the outer planets! This is one of the main reasons why I prefer to use the traditional planetary rulerships of the signs, because they lie within the boundary of Saturn, which helps us to stay grounded and relatively safe in the face of these great forces.

Each of the outer planets describes particular types of mass movements which threaten to swallow up our individuality:

> The change of character brought about by the uprush of collective forces is amazing. A gentle and reasonable being can be transformed into a maniac or a savage beast. One is always inclined to lay the blame on external circumstances, but nothing could explode in us if it had not been there. As a matter of fact, we are constantly living on the edge of a volcano, and there is, so far as we know, no way of protecting ourselves from a possible outburst that will destroy everybody within reach. It is certainly a good thing to preach reason and common sense, but what if you have a lunatic asylum

for an audience or a crowd in a collective frenzy? There is not much difference between them because the madman and the mob are both moved by impersonal, overwhelming forces.[2]

The zodiac signs in which the outer planets fall will describe the specific evolutionary potential of the period into which we are born. Uranus takes about seven years to pass through one sign of the zodiac. Neptune takes about 14 years and the elliptical Pluto takes from seven to 30 years. Each succeeding generation faces new challenges which were not relevant to previous generations. Indeed, as each generation grapples with the particular themes described by the signs in which the outer planets fall, it seems that subsequent generations are able to take for granted any increased awareness achieved by previous generations. The table below indicates the signs occupied by the outer planets over the last hundred years or so.

Although the outer planets primarily describe collective, generational, themes, when they make aspects to the personal and social planets the individuals concerned will be personally affected by collective, ancestral and archetypal themes and will, during their lives, act as carriers of, or channels for, these planetary principles. And as we will see next term, they are also of personal significance according to the astrological houses in which they occur and when they fall on an angle in an individual's birth chart.

	URANUS	NEPTUNE	PLUTO
Average Time Spent in a Sign	7 Years	14 Years	20 Years
ARIES	Apr 1927 Nov 1927* Jan 1928		
TAURUS	Sep 1934 Oct 1934* Mar 1935		
GEMINI	May 1942		
CANCER	June 1949	Jul 1901 Dec 1901* May 1902	Sep 1912 Oct 1912* Jul 1913 Dec 1913* May 1914

LEO	Aug 1955 Jan 1956* June 1956	Sep 1914 Dec 1914* July 1915 Mar 1916* May 1916	Oct 1937 Nov 1937* Aug 1938 Feb 1939* June 1939
VIRGO	Aug 1962	Sep 1928 Feb 1929* July 1929	Oct 1956 Jan 1957* Aug 1957 Apr 1958* June 1958
LIBRA	Sep 1968 May 1969* June 1969	Oct 1942 Apr 1943* Aug 1943	Oct 1971 Apr 1972* Jul 1972
SCORPIO	Nov 1974 May 1975* Sep 1975	Oct 1956 June 1957* Aug 1957	Nov 1983 May 1984* Aug 1984
SAGITTARIUS	Nov 1981	Nov 1970	Jan 1995 Apr 1995* Nov 1995
CAPRICORN	Feb 1988 May 1988* Dec 1988	Jan 1984 June 1984* Nov 1984	Jan 2008 June 2008* Nov 2008
AQUARIUS	Apr 1995 June 1995* Jan 1996	Jan 1998 Aug 1998* Nov 1998	
PISCES	Mar 2003 Sep 2003* Dec 2003	April 2011 Aug 2011* Feb 2012	
ARIES	May 2010 Aug 2010* Mar 2011		

* Planet retrograde, moves back into previous sign

URANUS

Uranus was discovered in 1781, by William Herschel, an organist and amateur astronomer living in Bath. Herschel discovered something completely unexpected – the existence of a planet lying outside the orbit of Saturn. Unlike all the other planets, with their horizontal equators rotating around vertical axes, Uranus has a more or less vertical equator rotating around a horizontal axis – so it spins virtually 90 degrees 'off

Uranus is ringed like Saturn, but rotates on a vertical axis.

centre' from the rest of the planets. Uranus breaks the rules – it is 'different', 'unusual', 'unexpected', 'eccentric' and 'shocking' – all key words for its astrological interpretation.

The second clue to the interpretation of Uranus is that its discovery was only possible because of scientific advances, and it was the development of the telescope which enabled this particular discovery and revealed a much larger cosmos than anyone had hitherto suspected. This discovery destroyed at a stroke the old world, the safe, contained solar system bounded by Saturn. The unexpected doubling of the size of the solar system created a kind of intellectual vertigo, a 'dizziness of freedom', a new faith in science and in the unlimited possibilities of the future. Since 1781 we have been living in a new world order, and the subsequent discoveries of Neptune and Pluto have expanded our solar system – and potentially our consciousness – even further.

The new planet was originally named after King George III, the politically inept king who suffered a breakdown in 1788 and eventually became violently insane. The planet was subsequently named after Uranus, the distant god of the starry heavens, but has increasingly come to be associated with the myth of Prometheus.³ It was Prometheus who stole fire from the gods for the benefit of mankind, and who was cruelly punished for his act of hubris. The relevance of this myth is that Prometheus had no respect for tradition or for authority and broke the established rules in the interests of human advancement. Prometheus symbolises the creative spark which leads to cultural and technological breakthrough, the enhancement of human autonomy, sudden enlightenment, and intellectual and spiritual awakening. This sacrilegious act gave mankind new powers which were previously the preserve of the gods, and the punishment for the crime of hubris or godlike inflation is

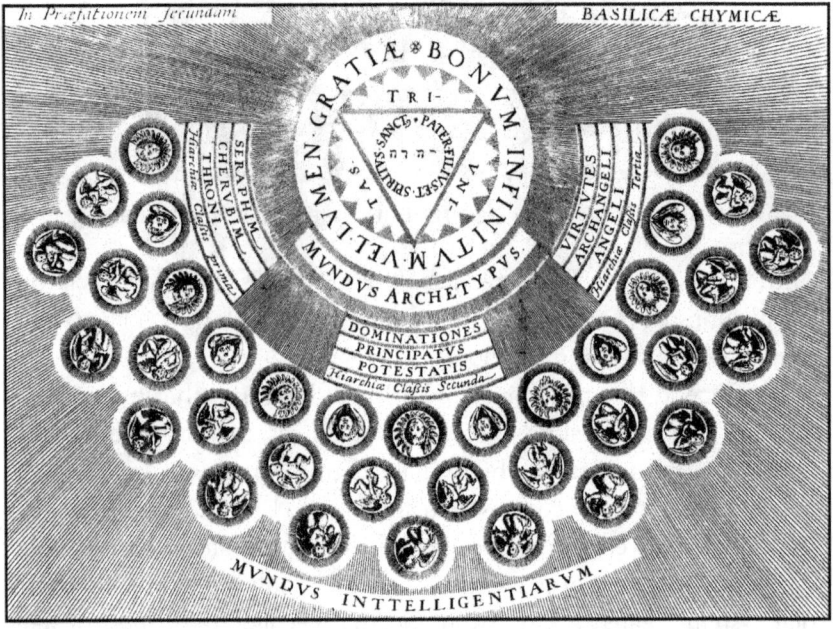

Uranus is not personified in alchemical texts, but as the "starry heavens" he is equated with the *mundus archetypus*, the Platonic world of Divine Ideas. This engraving, from *Opus medico-chymicum* by Johann Daniel Mylius (1618), portrays Divine Intelligence as radiant light descending through the realm of Ideas and the three classes of angelic hierarchies toward the world of form.

often swift and terrible. As Richard Tarnas has shown, it is not unusual for brilliant innovators and scientists who contribute significantly to our collective advancement to suffer dreadfully on a personal level.

The Synchronicity
The word 'synchronos' refers to events occurring at the same time which are not causally related. Since the outer planets are collective in their nature, we can learn a great deal about their meaning by examining the nature of the various mass movements which were occurring around the time of their discoveries. As far as Uranus is concerned, the following passage, written by a non-astrologer historian, illustrates this point:

> After 1789 there began to be the beginning of a new sort of revolution, a rupture with the past, characterised by violence, by limitless possibilities for fundamental change, social, political and economic. Men began to think, too, that this new phenomenon might transcend national boundaries and have something universal and general about it.[4]

The old order was being challenged by a completely new kind of radical, secular thinking which triggered many mass movements whose general theme was a utopian vision of creating a better future for all humanity. It was this kind of thinking which led not only to the French Revolution, but also to the American Declaration of Independence in 1776. At the same time, the industrial and scientific revolutions were under way, driven by scientific developments and a new faith that science could provide all the answers. The use of slogans, short, sharp messages designed to arrest our attention, are particularly Uranian phenomena, such as 'equality, freedom, brotherhood' or 'government of the people, by the people for the people'. More ominously, 'All pigs are equal, but some are more equal than others', from George Orwell's *Animal Farm*. This phrase illustrates that ideologies have their dark sides too, such as mass social manipulation by an elite few masquerading as the 'people's representatives'.

[At this moment, two events occur. One of the student's mobile phones starts to ring, and at the same time a stranger unexpectedly enters the room. She tells us she is looking for a video, which she extracts from the television in the room and then leaves.]

Audience: What was that all about?

Clare: We have just experienced an example of 'metalog', a phenomenon which occurs all the time when we are working with astrology. Basically, metalog means 'that which is being discussed is also arising'. It is an expression of the magical world which begins to come alive for us as we start thinking and living with an astrological awareness. Whenever we start discussing a particular planetary principle, we are also evoking that force as a living reality. Astrology is a living tradition, not something static or sterile. When we observe metalog in action we are making a connection to another dimension of reality which is not normally available to us until we have the language to understand it. Astrology is one of these languages.

Let me explain. First of all, a mobile phone started ringing and a woman simultaneously entered the room. Both of these events were unexpected, and it is always the unexpected which happens when Uranus is evoked. Now all technology, including mobile phones, videos and televisions, are ruled by Uranus. It is almost as if the principle of Uranus itself is seeking to communicate with us now that we have evoked it. This is something which happens all the time and which you will gradually get used to. Later on, when we start talking about Neptune, we will all lose it a bit and things will become fuzzy and rather confused. I was also thinking about the incident last week, when we were talking about Saturn. Do you remember the man who wanted to come into the room before the end of the class? We barred him from entering, since we had our space and time boundaries and were entitled to keep him out until the end of our class. In that case the boundaries remained intact. In this case, however, the Uranian energy broke straight into the room ignoring the rules and regulations, which is typical of the planet Uranus!

There are many examples of the way Uranus functions. Town planning and architecture in England in the 1960s, for example, was driven by ideals of creating a better life for the ordinary people. Throughout the country the old slums were cleared away and, often in spite of strong resistance, people were rehoused in new tower blocks. The utopian vision was that the lot of ordinary people would be improved if they were living high in the sky in a kind of clean symmetry, rather than in the dirty, crowded, chaotic slums. Ordinary human emotions were never considered, and the vision began to crumble as the old sense of community was destroyed and the tower blocks gradually came to be associated with new levels of social isolation, crime and intimidation which had never existed before.

There is often a fanatical and brutal edge to Uranian ideals which can cause great misery and unhappiness if ordinary human emotions are not taken into consideration. The population control measures in China are an example of draconian rules designed for the benefit of the country as a whole which ride roughshod over ordinary human concerns. However rational and logical it may be for China to restrict its population growth, it is unlikely that the Chinese couple restricted to having one child only would agree that this planet of liberation and opportunity has set them free. Hunger strikes and the more recent phenomena of suicide bombers are examples of the shocking and uncompromising way that individuals sacrifice themselves, or are sacrificed to, political causes.

Uranus rules social and political engineering, such as positive discrimination, and although this may well be beneficial to some extent, it also has a darker face too. The practice of eugenics, the creation of a perfect master race and the elimination of anyone who does not fit the current arbitrary criteria of perfection, as implemented by the Nazis against the Jews, is an example of collective Uranian insanity.

Uranus in the Birth Chart
Uranus is the principle of rebellion, ideology, alienation, eccentricity, deviation from the norm, perversity, intellectual clarity and brilliance, scientific invention, idealism, brainwaves, breakthrough and magnetism. Uranus is restless, disruptive and shocking, cut off from ordinary human emotions. Uranus rules scientists, astronomers, radiographers, inventors, revolutionaries, anarchists, politicians and in the mundane world, television stations, electricity, radio waves, computers, new technology, laser beams, magnetic fields, telepathy and satellites.

Uranus gives us access to intuitive flashes of knowledge or revelation that come from outside our conscious awareness. In the birth chart, Uranus gives us detachment and perspective. It describes how and where we are intellectually idealistic, and seek to break down the old order and create a more perfect world for the benefit of all. On the other hand, if we identify with Uranus we can become dominated by an ideology or by what we believe to be an 'ultimate truth', which is used to justify our actions. Uranus rules both genius and insanity. Like electricity, it is not safe unless it is earthed.

Audience: Uranus sounds like an extremely aggressive planet?

Clare: It is certainly aggressive to the extent that the concerns, values and lives of ordinary people are ignored in the interests of cultural, political and universal advancement. In this sense it is not so much aggressive as ruthless, and Uranus in our own charts describes how and where we ourselves can be ruthless and cut off from human emotions.

The sign in which Uranus is placed describes in what way an entire group of people born within a seven year period will rebel and react against the norm. What is interesting about this is that when we rebel and react against something, then it has us in its grip and we are not free of it. We can become dominated and alienated by a kind of 'group think' to the extent that we lose our individuality. For example, we might say 'I am a communist', rather than 'I am an individual with communist ideals'. I don't know if that makes sense to you?

Audience: So Uranus takes us over and makes us behave in a rebellious way?

Clare: Yes, that's exactly the point. It can become such a powerful force in our lives that we can even be prepared to die for a particular ideal or vision. The principle becomes more important than our own lives. We can be gripped by a collective ideology which will destroy us. Although it is not appropriate to judge whether this is a good or a bad thing, nevertheless there is no doubt that on an ordinary personal level this is likely to create tremendous suffering.

Audience: What happens if our personal planets make aspects to the outer planets? Is there any hope for us then?

Clare: Whether or not we have personal planets in aspect to Uranus, we all have Uranus somewhere in our charts, so to some extent we will inevitably get caught up in the collective thinking of our generation. The question is whether the collective thinking takes us over to the extent that we lose our humanity.

Audience: But I always thought that Uranus was the planet of individuality?

Clare: This is a very common misunderstanding until we learn that there is nothing individual about the outer planets or about the mass movements associated with them. It is important to differentiate between 'individuality' and 'deviation or alienation from the norm'. Uranians, who would be people with several planets in Aquarius or the planet Uranus angular or strongly aspected in their birth chart, tend to have a vision or a way of thinking which deviates from the norm and, as a result they often feel like misfits or aliens in some way. A perfectly understandable reaction is to cut off and adopt the attitude that 'I don't want to belong anyway', which is not the same thing at all as individuality, but a wounded response to being excluded or singled out as 'odd' in some way. Everyone born within a particular seven year period will be part of a collective ideology or 'group think' which challenges the meaning of the sign it is in and, in the process, brings new ideas and new ideologies and breakthroughs relating to that particular sign.

Aspects to Uranus
Have a look at the charts of the two case studies we will be using this term. Both David and Sally have **Sun-Uranus** aspects. The Sun-Uranus aspect is autocratic, describing people who refuse to conform or to toe the line. Sun-Uranus individuals are not group players, except on their own terms. This is a high voltage, magnetic contact, often found in the charts of individuals who are ahead of their time, intellectually brilliant, inventive, radical, reactionary, detached and non-conformist.

With her **Venus-Uranus** aspect, Sally will value (Venus) her freedom and autonomy (Uranus). She may be prone to sudden, unexpected (Uranus) attractions (Venus), and to unconventional (Uranus) relationships (Venus). Sally will value (Venus) friendship, equality and truthfulness (Uranus) both in herself and in others. She may also be attracted to (Venus) art and music (Venus) which is shocking or arresting (Uranus) in some way. How would you interpret a **Moon-Uranus** contact?

Audience: Could this be an unusual or unpredictable or unstable mother?

Clare: Yes, it could describe a woman who is ambivalent (Uranus) about motherhood (Moon), or someone who has had inconsistent (Uranus) mothering (Moon). It can also describe scientific involvement (Uranus) in the process of conception (Moon), such as *in vitro* fertilisation. It can also describe a woman (Moon) ahead of her time (Uranus), such as Marie Curie or Mary Woollstoncroft. There may have been many early disruptions (Uranus) in the family (Moon), or being cut off from or separated from (Uranus) one's family (Moon) in some way. There is a strong need (Moon) for freedom and space (Uranus), a need (Moon) to rebel and to shock (Uranus). It can also indicate someone who is cut off from (Uranus) their feelings (Moon).

NEPTUNE

Neptune was first sighted in 1846, although there has always been some confusion about who actually discovered it. From the behaviour of the orbit of Uranus, it was known that another planet existed outside the orbit of Uranus and the two mathematicians, the English John Adams and the French Urbain Leverrier both predicted the correct position where it would be found. The planet was named after Poseidon, Neptune, god of the sea.

The Synchronicity

The mid–19th century saw the emergence of mass movements of a humanitarian nature and the development of organisations concerned with the institutionalised care of the masses. To some extent this movement can be seen as a reaction to the suffering caused by the radical advances occurring at the time of the discovery of Uranus. There began to be a new collective awareness that, for example, people should not be allowed to just die on the streets. The welfare of the poor became a matter of public concern, and hospitals and 'poor houses' for the needy were set up. Slavery was abolished in the US in 1861, the same year that the bond labour of the serfs in Russia came to an end, and mining legislation was introduced in the UK. The rise of socialism led to the formation of trades unions and workers cooperatives and in 1848 Karl Marx's *Com-*

munist Manifesto was published. We could say that Uranus and Neptune symbolise right wing and left wing ends of the political spectrum.

Towards the end of the 19th century there was a remarkable growth of interest in the occult and in spiritualism, and all over Europe people were holding séances, conjuring disembodied entities, table-rapping, manifesting ectoplasm and goodness knows what else. Naturally, many of these phenomena were deliberate illusions and tricks, which is appropriate to our theme, since Neptune rules prevailing fashions,

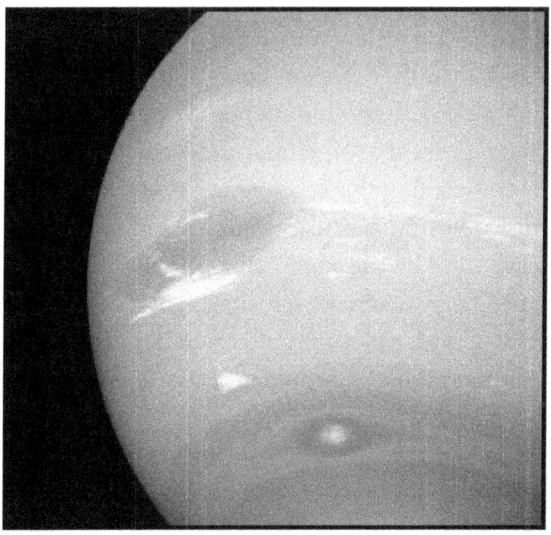

dreams, fantasies, illusions and deception. On the other hand Neptune's function is to dissolve the boundaries between our ordinary lives and other realms of existence. The theosophical movement established by Madame Blavatsky was one example of the growing resistance to the rationalism and materialism of the previous century. Two major features of the theosophical movement were the telepathic communications of a mystical Tibetan brotherhood working for the salvation of humanity, and the search for the new avatar or saviour who was presumed to be living somewhere in India.

This was also the time of the Californian and Australian gold rushes, in which thousands of people were gripped by the collective dream of amassing great personal wealth. Wherever Neptune is involved, it is the dream and the fantasy which has us in its grip, rather than the actual reality. The gold rushes subsided on a tide of disillusionment almost as quickly as they had emerged, leaving a trail of ghost towns in their wake. The music and art of the 19th century tends to be fluid, romantic and dreamy. If you think of the music of Debussy and Chopin, the art of Fragonard, Constable and Turner and the poetry of Wordsworth, you can easily conjure up the atmosphere of this period.

Neptune rules everything which is atmospherically powerful but physically invisible or intangible, such as the steam which was increasingly being used to generate power for industry and transport, and the gas which began to be used for lighting. New drugs were being discovered and anaesthetics were being introduced to reduce pain. As a general rule we could say that Neptune's function is to take our pain away, by whatever means. Neptune rules religion. It is the anaesthetic which relieves the pain of separation and isolation.

So Neptune rules the sea, its colours are soft greens and blues. It rules plants that live in or by the water, all marine life, fish and fishmongers.

It rules people who create illusions, such as photographers, film-makers, dancers and actors. In the mundane world, Neptune rules hospitals, prisons and breweries, oil and floods, drugs, poisons, biological weapons and alcohol.

Audience: What about psychics and mediums and people who do divination, using the tarot for example? Presumably these are Neptunian things, but are they really channelling information from other worlds?

Clare: This is an interesting question. How do we know if they have just lost the plot or if they are truly in touch with some kind of higher level of knowledge and wisdom?

Audience: But what is the answer? How can you recognise the difference?

Clare: I think that it is very, very hard to answer that. Neptune teaches us that there are parallel realities and other worlds, and who is to say which of the worlds is real? Where Neptune is concerned, we cannot judge which of us are mad and deluded, and which of us are sane. The point about Neptune is that the truth is whatever you want it to be.

The Outer Planets 79

Although Neptune and Pluto were unknown as planets in the 17th century, this alchemical image, from *Escalier des sages* (1689) by Barent Coenders van Helpen, portrays Neptune (right, with Pluto on the left) representing the watery darkness of the primordial substance. Jupiter appears in the form of a swan, bringing the whiteness to the tincture, which heralds the advent of the Sun; the horses of the solar chariot are already in sight.

There is no doubt that the world is full of charlatans and confidence tricksters, people whose whole living is based upon creating false illusions. On the other hand, the world is full of beauty and meaning and experiences of the divine which can inspire extraordinary devotion and acts of tremendous compassion and kindness.

Neptune in the Birth Chart
Neptune is the principle of devotion, transcendence, refinement, redemption, surrender, enchantment, glamour, longing, disillusion, chaos, deception and escapism. In the birth chart, Neptune describes how and where we long to merge with and dissolve into something greater than ourselves. Neptune is where we give ourselves away and where we refuse to acknowledge boundaries. It also describes where we are likely to be unrealistic, unfocussed and evasive, where we deceive ourselves and others, where we can end up feeling betrayed and disillusioned.

Neptune's urge is deeply religious and mystical. It is our capacity for unconditional and joyful devotion, compassion and empathy, our ability to give of ourselves without wanting anything in return. It is where we have access to magical worlds of perfect enchantment, and where we can become channels for the expression of overwhelming beauty and divine ideals. Neptune connects us to the sublime. Think of composers such as Mozart or Bach, whose music poured through them and gives people immense joy. Neptune can describe our service to mankind, for the benefit of the collective. Without Neptune in our charts we would have to live without our fantasies or dreams, which would, of course, be unthinkable.

Audience: Did you say that Neptune rules drugs and alcohol?

Clare: That's right. Addictions are a way of escaping from the hard edges of the world.

Audience: So we can never find satisfaction where Neptune is?

Clare: I think we can find satisfaction provided we don't want anything for ourselves. Neptune describes a genuine connection to something greater than us, but if we try to benefit personally from this connection, then we will never feel satisfied because we always want more. This is the basis of addictions because the more we have the more we want and we are always unsatisfied. This is where Neptune can be literally self-destructive.

Audience: So it is an unfulfilled hunger.

Clare: Exactly, to the extent that we want something for ourselves and to the extent that the ego has an agenda. But if we can find the right relationship to this planet, its more destructive expressions of inflation, dissatisfaction and addiction to our own suffering, do not have to become a feature in our lives.

Audience: Isn't it dangerous to have no boundaries?

Clare: There is an understandable fear that we will lose ourselves altogether if we give of ourselves unconditionally. But this is the ego's fear.
Provided we have a strong, well developed personal container, or ego structure, then we will not be overwhelmed by the forces of the outer planets because we have a choice. There is all the difference between Neptune living us, and us living Neptune, if you see what I mean. If we actually make a personal choice to devote ourselves unconditionally to something, then we don't have to be drowned or dissolved, used, abused and burned out. It is the ability to choose, which means that Neptune doesn't have to drain the life force out of us.

Audience: So if you really know your chart and you have a good sense of who you are, then you are able to give where Neptune is?

Clare: Yes. Let's go back to basics. If we can meet our basic needs for ourselves (Moon), if we know our own minds (Mercury), if we are basically fulfilled and having some fun (Venus), if we have the ability to assert and defend ourselves when necessary (Mars), and engage fully and successfully with the world around us (Jupiter and Saturn), then we will have developed a good strong ego-structure which protects us from being taken over by the collective forces symbolised by the outer planets.

Audience: But it can be incredibly difficult just to develop a good enough ego.

Clare: That's right, and I think that it is our major task, as psychological astrologers, to work on redeeming and empowering the seven traditional planets in our own charts and in the charts of our clients. The outer planets can take care of themselves. For example, it is a hopeless task to try and get our personal gratification through Neptune. But we can certainly get this through Venus. And we will always be vulnerable to being overwhelmed by collective forces until we have consciously integrated Saturn, which will keep us safe on a personal level.

Audience: So until then you are not really equipped to handle the outer planets?

Clare: At the end of the day we are all muddling along, trying to make the best of our lives and, using an astrological approach, learning to take responsibility for ourselves so that we can make a positive difference in our own lives and in the lives of others. But I think it is true to say that, since the discovery of Uranus, the old rules and certainties have started to break down. People's lives are no longer defined or safely contained within church and state in the way they used to be. Society used to be a container for the individual, but we now have to become our own containers. We have become so collective tonight that we are in danger of losing ourselves, which is something that always happens when Neptune is evoked. Things get clearer and easier to manage when we put Neptune into the birth chart and link it to the other planets. Then we can begin to get a handle on the way Neptune is likely to express itself in an individual's life, which can have a wide range of expression all the way from an immense sensitivity to beauty and perfection, to spirituality, to addiction and self destructiveness. We need to ground Neptune into a birth chart in order to make progress with it.

Neptune Aspects
Sally has a **Sun-Neptune** aspect, so we would anticipate that her father (Sun) was in some sense elusive, out of reach, physically or psychologically absent (Neptune). This can set up a longing (Neptune) for the father

(Sun), an unrealistic idealisation (Neptune) of the masculine (Sun), and unrealistic expectations (Neptune) of herself (Sun). Unless she has a strong enough ego, Sally may be prone to confusion and evasiveness, a lack of personal boundaries and a refusal to commit (Neptune). She may find that she is constantly exhausted and overwhelmed (Neptune) by the demands of the world and of others. Ultimately, however, she is a sensitive, gentle and compassionate soul (Neptune) who can find fulfilment and joy (Sun) by channelling her talents and natural capacity for empathy into creative artistic expression or by devoting herself to the needs of others.

David's Neptune makes aspects to Mercury, Venus, Mars and Saturn. The **Mercury-Neptune** aspect describes a poetic and imaginative (Neptune) mind (Mercury). To the extent that Neptune is in control, he may find it difficult to concentrate (Neptune) or to think clearly (Mercury), preferring to live in a fantasy world of his own making. His thinking process (Mercury) may be confused and chaotic (Neptune), and he may become evasive or deceitful (Neptune) in order to avoid having to face up to the truth. He may even deliberately manipulate others by spinning illusions and fantasies (Neptune) and making promises (Mercury) which he has no intention of honouring. On the other hand, if he has a strong enough sense of identity, this contact is extremely imaginative and poetic. David could be a wonderful storyteller (Mercury), musician or artist (Neptune) with the gift to inspire people by taking them into magical worlds of fantasy.

Neptune-Venus can indicate an unfulfilled longing for or addiction (Neptune) to love (Venus) which is never satisfied. If Neptune is in control, David could be evasive and deceitful (Neptune) in relationships (Venus), unable to feel fulfilled and always thirsty for and longing for something or someone more perfect (Neptune). He will be unable to relate realistically (Venus) to himself or to others and could become addicted to his own suffering (Neptune). With a good enough ego structure, this contact is immensely gifted and artistic (Venus), and David will have a heightened appreciation (Neptune) of beauty and peace (Venus), the ability to touch the divine (Neptune) and to serve with unconditional devotion (Neptune) and joy (Venus).

Neptune-Mars can describe the ideal or illusion or fantasy (Neptune) of strength and potency (Mars). Unless there is a relatively well formed ego structure and a well developed personal Mars, David may feel extremely vulnerable and weak (Neptune), afraid of being attacked (Mars), easily intimidated and unable to stand up for or defend himself. The positive expression of Neptune-Mars is the ability to use his energy (Mars) with sensitivity and subtlety (Neptune), to navigate the waters (Neptune) in a skilful and effective way (Mars). The combination of sensitivity (Neptune) and focus (Mars) can be immensely effective, and is often found on the charts of racing yachtsmen, artists or dancers.

A **Neptune-Saturn** aspect brings together two very different principles, since Saturn describes boundaries, containment and practical reality, and Neptune has no boundaries, is uncontained and not of this world. For so long as the ego structure remains diffuse and unformed (Neptune), Neptune is likely to undermine and dissolve (Neptune) any sense of safety or containment (Saturn), and overwhelm the ego (Saturn) with unrealistic dreams and expectations (Neptune). Working positively together, Saturn can turn the highest principles and values of Neptune into reality, give shape and form (Saturn) to the divine (Neptune), enable an individual to work (Saturn) for and serve the greater good (Neptune) and to ground (Saturn) their dreams and ideals (Neptune) so that they can be made manifest in the world (Saturn).

PLUTO

The time has come to have a look at Pluto – we are certainly having a rather heavy evening tonight. The existence of Pluto was established mathematically in 1915 by the astronomer Percival Lowall, working in Arizona, although it was actually first sighted in 1930 after Lowall's death. It is inclined to the orbital plane of the other planets by up to 17 degrees and has a pronounced elliptical orbit, which means that it travels much faster through some signs than through others. With an average period of 20 years in a sign, it actually takes approximately 30 years to transit through the sign of Taurus, when it is at its greatest distance from the Sun, and approximately seven years to transit through the sign of Scorpio, when it is at its closest to the Sun and inside the orbit of Neptune.

Audience: I knew there was something weird about Pluto. It's also very small, isn't it? There is a model of the relative sizes of all the planets at the London Planetarium. I remember seeing Pluto and thinking that it was really, really small. You get the Earth and Venus and Mars, which are all broadly the same size, although the Moon is smaller, and then you get to the huge planets of Jupiter and Saturn, and then you walk on past Saturn to Uranus and Neptune until you get to this very tiny planet, Pluto.

Clare: Yes, it's very small and very dark. Apparently it is one tenth of the expected brightness for its size, so it is considered to be very dense, swallowing light.

Audience: It sounds like a black hole.

Clare: Yes, this is an excellent image for Pluto, a symbol of condensed and concentrated power. In Greek mythology, Hades or Pluto was immensely powerful and wealthy, the god of buried treasure and of the underworld, where the souls of the dead reside. I am sure you are familiar with the myth of Persephone, who was forcibly abducted by Pluto and snatched away into the underworld. Symbolically, Pluto describes a

forced initiation which appears to come out of nowhere, but changes our lives forever. It is where we are taken over by forces we never believed we were going to get involved with.

It is interesting that there is an ongoing debate about whether Pluto is in fact a planet at all, or whether it should be classified as belonging to the Kuiper Belt. From a psychological perspective, if Pluto does not belong in the solar system then it doesn't belong within the human psyche, and we don't have to take responsibility for it as an aspect of ourselves. Perhaps it is not surprising, therefore, that the astronomers are trying to get it removed. An interesting development is that Pluto is in fact a binary system with a moon which is approximately the same size. This moon is called Charon, the ferryman in Greek myth, who rowed people over the river Styx into the land of the dead in exchange for a piece of silver. This seems to me to be a rather important discovery from a symbolic point of view. Now that we have discovered Charon we have a link to Pluto – a vessel in which to travel to Hades. We can get there, but we will have to pay the price.

The Synchronicity
In common with the other outer planets, Pluto has come to be associated with the particular types of mass movements which were occurring around the time of its discovery. This was the era which saw the rise of a group of extraordinarily powerful, brutal, charismatic dictators who carried enormous collective power. In 1930, for example, Stalin collectivised the farms and instigated the purges against Trotsky's supporters. Purging is a very powerful Pluto word, meaning to raze something to the ground, to annihilate something with the purpose of purifying it. Mao Tse Tung's communist revolution began with his Long March in 1934, during which 100,000 people perished, and at the same time the fascist leaders Mussolini and Hitler came to power in Europe. In one year, between 1928 and 1929, for example, the Nazi vote rose from 800,000 to 6,409,000. Between them, these leaders, who could also be described as megalomaniacs, were the cause of literally millions of deaths, often of their own people.

Audience: So you are saying that when these outer planets are first identified, then it is time for them to come into mass consciousness?

Pluto, in an alchemical engraving from *Escalier des sages* by Barent Coenders van Helpen (1689), holds the key to the alchemical operation of *putrefactio*, which opens the door to the underworld and makes possible the transformation of the primal substance. Neptune reclines on the ground beside him.

Clare: Exactly. What we can certainly say is that, before this time, nothing like this had ever occurred on this kind of scale or intensity.

Audience: It seems as if the energy of these new planets is much more intense around their discovery, and then it dies away. Maybe all the stored up unconscious energy has to burst out when a new planet is discovered.

Clare: Yes, this certainly seems to be the case. There are other movements which belong to this period which reflect similar themes of brutal power, great wealth, control and crisis. For example, prohibition throughout the USA during the 1920s is often associated with the mafia. The film *Road to Perdition* is an excellent portrayal of the dark power of the mafia during those times. The Wall Street Crash of 1929 wiped out $26 billion, causing a global economic crisis. And yet, out of the rubble, in 1930, the Empire State Building was built in an astonishingly short period of time. The splitting of the atom released enormous power, and coincided with the foundation of modern depth psychology, pioneered by Freud. Freud's psychic archaeology involved delving into the unconscious to discover repressed and buried material. The task he set himself was the excavation of the buried contents of the unconscious and the release of the suppressed life force which enabled his patients to experience psychic healing and a profound experience of rebirth. These themes were also reflected in the arts. The romanticism of the mid–nineteenth century gave way to the surrealism and to new images of a harsh, dismembered, fragmented and deconstructed world, given expression in the work of Picasso and others. Jazz replaced the romantic music of the 19th century composers such as Debussy.

Pluto rules anything that is underground: potholers, power stations, secret societies, political underground movements, volcanoes, earthquakes, depth psychology, liquidators, detectives, anything to do with waste, recycling, sewage works, bodily elimination and sexuality. In short, Pluto rules all things which are dark, buried and taboo, the things that no-one wants to think about or talk about. Collectively, Pluto concerns the organic laws of decay, death and regeneration of all living things in the interests of collective survival.

Pluto in the Birth Chart

As an invisible force, Pluto has to be experienced before we can truly understand and appreciate its power. We cannot grasp its meaning from a distance or with our intellects because it is so primal and primitive. Pluto is a deep reservoir of concentrated power in our birth charts, which can remain dormant for a long time, like a volcano. In its dormant phase, it tends to be a dumb note in the birth chart and it is perfectly possible to live for long periods as if it didn't exist. If we mention issues of power and control to people in their dormant Pluto phase they are unlikely to know what we are talking about.

In its active phase, however, Pluto will start to rumble and the intensity will start to build deep in the unconscious until the tension and intensity of the suppressed energy becomes unbearable. The power of the feelings which are eventually unleashed can take us completely by surprise. Pluto undermines our sense of ourselves as civilised and reasonable human beings and plunges us into what can feel like an alien and terrifying underworld of savage emotions such as rage, jealousy, obsession, vengeance, power battles, control issues, survival anxiety and murderousness.

When Pluto is activated it is obsessive and compulsive, and pulls everything towards it, like a black hole. At root, Pluto describes the life force itself, the urge to bring to the surface and eliminate anything which no longer serves life because it has become poisonous, decayed or rotten. Pluto purges and regenerates. If we can surrender to this process, and we often have no choice in the matter, then we can experience Pluto's healing and cleansing power for ourselves. Naturally, we never choose this, since Pluto's function is to take us to hell and back. Pluto is the principle of intensity, catharsis, power and control, purging, regeneration and collective survival. It describes how and where we feel compelled to fight for our personal survival, where we are obsessive and how we sabotage ourselves and others in an effort to maintain control.

For so long as we ignore Pluto by trying to control it or by denying its existence in our chart, we will deny the primitive, savage, dark and destructive aspects of our nature, with the result that we will project these qualities onto others or onto the outside world. Once Pluto is activated, however, it describes how and where the individual can be the vessel through which that which is poisonous and destructive in the collective can be purged, healed and cleansed. If we consciously accept the challenge of Pluto in our charts, we can cooperate with the process of psychic purging which is a necessary prerequisite to any genuine self healing.

Audience: So we are still struggling with accepting responsibility for it?

Clare: Yes. For so long as we are identified with an image of ourselves as perfectly civilised, righteous and upstanding people, then we need others to carry the darkness or evil for us. This will enable us to keep to our moral high grounds and be outraged by the terrible deeds and behaviour of others, and we will continue looking for and seeing and even creating the darkness 'out there' until we can each carry the burden of our own potential for savage, brutal behaviour.

Pluto Aspects

Both Sally and David have **Pluto-Sun** aspects, which indicate personal (Sun) intensity (Pluto) and survival issues. Sometimes the individual's real identity (Sun) is hidden from them (Pluto), to the extent that they develop a 'false self' or false identity, which protects them from exposure (Pluto), but also keeps them hidden (Pluto) from themselves (Sun). From the ego's perspective, the individual is likely to feel vulnerable and open to attack, even to the point of paranoia (Pluto). They will find it impossible to trust, and will seek to maintain control over others at all times. Ultimately, the Sun-Pluto person is challenged to surrender his or her compulsion for personal control, and become a conduit through which the life force itself is purged, regenerated and released.

Pluto-Moon describes an intensely (Pluto) emotional and instinctive nature (Moon). If the ego is involved, Sally is likely to be possessive, devouring and emotionally invasive, to the extent that anyone who lands on her spider's web will be trapped, bound by emotional (Moon) blackmail (Pluto) and unable to escape. She is equally capable of destroying or healing (Pluto) herself and others on a powerful psychic level (Moon). With this aspect devoted to the service of others, rather than to her own needs, she will not be afraid to put her life on the line in the interests of healing and nurturing others and setting them free.

Pluto-Venus indicates that Sally will have an intense (Pluto) desire nature (Venus), and an attraction (Venus) to hidden, taboo relationships (Pluto). For so long as this aspect is functioning in an ego-centric manner, Sally may use her undoubted powers of attraction (Venus) to control, ensnare, seduce, manipulate and destroy others. Positively, this aspect describes Sally's capacity to go through hell and back (Pluto) for what she values (Venus), without fears for her own safety, to fight for others who are, for example, sexually (Venus) exploited (Pluto), to devote herself to healing (Pluto) people with sexually transmitted (Venus) diseases (Pluto), or to force taboo sexual practices (Pluto) to the surface so that they can be eliminated (Pluto).

The **Pluto-Mercury** contact in David's chart describes the power (Pluto) of language (Mercury), the compulsion (Pluto) to give voice (Mercury) to what is taboo or secret in order to defuse its hidden power (Pluto). If the interests of the ego are involved, this aspect can describe interrogation, the use of verbal (Mercury) intimidation and manipulation (Pluto) of others for one's own benefit. One way of doing this is by being totally silent (Mercury-Pluto), which can be a way of manipulating people into speaking first and therefore exposing themselves.

An individual with a **Pluto-Mars** contact never seems to feel alive unless they are fighting (Mars) for their personal survival (Pluto) or have put their lives on the line in some way. They tend to take themselves to the edge (Mars), which is where they feel truly alive (Pluto). This is an excellent combination for a racing driver or for a member of the SAS, anyone who challenges themselves (Mars) to survive (Pluto). Tremendously driven and determined, these people come alive (Mars) in a crisis (Pluto). If the interests of the ego are involved, this aspect describes the use of brutal force (Mars) and control (Pluto) over others for personal benefit. The most positive expression of this aspect is the power and determination and courage to put one's life on the line for the benefit of others and for the healing of the collective.

CHIRON

Discovered in 1977 by the astronomer Charles Koval in Pasadena, California, Chiron has been described as a 'planetoid' or as a trapped comet, most probably originating from the Kuiper Belt. Its orbital period is between 49-51 years, but the question remains whether it is a temporary visitor to the solar system and, if so, for how long it will be with us. The answer is we don't know, because it was only discovered less than 30 years ago. I would certainly recommend that you read Melanie Reinhart's excellent book on Chiron and the centaurs.[5]

Audience: Is this possible that the planets could also leave their orbits?

Clare: Planets are caught firmly in the gravitational field of the Sun, but comets have a much more tenuous connection. They are considered to originate in the Kuiper Belt outside the solar system, which they visit from time to time. Chiron is one of many bodies in our solar system which are now called centaurs – in fact a whole herd of them has now been discovered. Chiron was the first and, like Pluto, it has an extremely elliptical orbit. This means that it spends a great deal more time in some signs than others.

Audience: Has Chiron now been completely integrated into astrology?

Clare: No, not at all. There are many astrologers who don't use Chiron at all, which is of significance in itself, since Chiron is a maverick, it is not accepted and it doesn't belong. However, for psychologically inclined astrologers, I believe that Chiron is proving to be very meaningful. My own explanation for this is that Chiron only becomes real for us when we actually experience it for ourselves. In this sense it is similar to Pluto. As a concept, we can take it or leave it, but as an experience there is no doubt that it is profoundly significant. Having said that, I completely accept that there will continue to be a resistance to including Chiron in the birth chart, because it is painful to the ego, and can be humbling and humiliating. However, in the same way as the outer planets, now that it has been discovered out there in the solar system, we know that it also exists within the human psyche. So the question is what is it doing there and what does it have to teach us.

In Greek myth Chiron was a centaur, with the torso of a man and the body of a horse. Chiron was a wise teacher, who taught music, mathematics, astronomy, the art of war, medicine and all the other arts and sciences to the sons and daughters of the gods on Mount Olympus. He was also a particularly gifted healer. However, centaurs are rowdy

Chiron, photographed in 1995

creatures, particularly under the influence of alcohol, and easily get themselves into wild fights and brawls. At a particular wedding feast to which the centaurs were invited, a brawl developed and one of Hercules' poison tipped arrows accidentally became embedded in Chiron's thigh. The point about this story is that, although Chiron was a wonderful healer, he could not heal his own wound, no matter how hard he tried. This is the basis of the myth of the wounded healer and of the phrase 'physician, heal thyself'. After a tremendous amount of suffering, from which Chiron was unable to die, since, as the son of Zeus, he was immortal, he chose to exchange places with Prometheus, who had been chained to a rock as a punishment for stealing fire from the gods for the benefit of mankind. This exchange enabled him to surrender his immortality and die. After his death, he was cast in the heavens as the constellation of Centaurus.

This myth has much depth and is of great astrological significance. Like the centaurs, we ourselves are part animal, instinctive and mortal, and part immortal and spiritual. It is significant that the poisoned arrow pierced the thigh, the animal part of Chiron. The myth indicates that it is our animal bodies which are injured, and Chiron in the chart indicates where we have the potential to reconnect and to integrate our pure spiritual awareness with our dark animal wisdom. The last few hundred years has seen the tremendous explosion of scientific developments, which have enabled the human race to harness the world's resources for

Chiron is portrayed in this Roman fresco as the teacher of the hero Achilles. The wise centaur is not part of the iconography of alchemy, but the element of sulphur – the active, masculine component in the *opus* – is referred to in alchemical texts as the medicus or "wounded physician".

its own benefit. We have even started to fight against our own mortality, with the Uranian development of cryogenics. We are investing heavily in cloning and stem cell research and, although these developments are entirely logical in terms of the Uranian vision, they completely miss the point from the Chiron point of view.

It was not until the 1970s that a collective awareness emerged that our scientific and ecological developments could be damaging to our planet and to our bodies and that there may be a high price to pay. There was a new awareness of the fragility of the world, a new awareness that the food we were eating, the water we were drinking, the medications we were taking, the power cables running over our heads, could be poisoning our bodies.

Audience: Did this only start in the 1970s?

Clare: It is hard to realise now that there were times when it was taken for granted that all scientific developments were positive and that the Earth's natural resources could be exploited for our benefit, with no consequences. The theme of Chiron describes the price we pay for thinking that we are immortal and all-powerful and in full control of ourselves and of the world. In the end we cannot live as immortals, dissociated from our animal bodies. In some ways, Chiron could be seen as the evolution of a kind of dark wisdom which is the counterpart of the brilliance and clarity of Uranian insight. It is the animal part of ourselves which is flawed, because it suffers and because it is mortal. Chiron is therefore our Achilles heel, the part of us which can't be healed, and where, ultimately, we need to accept our imperfections and develop compassion for ourselves and for others.

In the birth chart, Chiron indicates where and how we feel awkward and flawed and where we feel as if we are not accepted or acceptable. In this sense, Chiron also describes where and how we are likely to be scapegoated by the group, where we expose the imperfections which the group is denying and are therefore blamed and excluded. There is a strong connection between Chiron and the shamanic calling. In all cultures and groups there have always been and still are shamanic figures who suffer the burdens and ills of the clan or group, and function as the group's healer. So Chiron in the chart is where we both suffer and heal, but the healing is for the benefit of others, not for ourselves.

Audience: There seem to be parallels here to the American Indians and to the Australian Aborigines. In both cases, they are very spiritually evolved, ecologically aware people with tremendous healing skills and crafts, and they have had their land taken away and their souls destroyed by the white settlers.

Clare: Perhaps it is significant that, since the discovery of Chiron, we are finally becoming aware of the value and wisdom of the knowledge of the aboriginal peoples all over the world. There is certainly a great deal of interest now in learning about and preserving the strong connection to nature and the healing wisdom of these peoples.

Audience: Can you say a bit more about the wounding and healing? Surely these are two very different things?

Clare: According to the law of opposites, which is so central to astrological and psychological thinking, the fact that they are opposites means that they are intimately connected and dependent upon each other. This is why we use the term 'the wounded healer'. Just to make things more complicated, I think it is more appropriate to see Chiron in terms of a triangular relationship between the wounded, the healer and the wounder. They are all aspects of the same thing. So, Chiron is wounded in the sense that this is where we are alienated, cast out, victimised and blamed. But it is because of this that Chiron also has particular healing gifts, because we can only be truly compassionate (which means to 'feel with') when we can truly relate to another person's suffering because it is our own suffering too. But this is also where we are capable of wounding others, because, like animals, we are extremely vulnerable when wounded and likely to lash out and attack as a way of defending ourselves. This is a fairly complex triangle, but well worth bearing in mind.

Audience: How can we relate Chiron's decision to die to our own situation? What does this actually mean when we interpret Chiron in the birth chart?

Clare: I think it is important to look at this symbolically because what eventually dies is our need to heal ourselves, our need to be perfect and flawless and our need to be accepted. In a way, Chiron in the chart describes where our ego control needs to be surrendered. In the process, we learn to be loyal to our own instinctual natures. Chiron spent a great deal of time and energy trying to heal himself, which is what we all try to do where Chiron is in our charts, because it is such a deeply sensitive point. We try to force ourselves to perform, to be strong and powerful where our Chiron is. For so long as we are still trying to 'fix it', we are likely to actually make it worse, and become more defensive or aggressive. Eventually, if we are fortunate, we will give up the pointless task and learn to accept ourselves just as we are.

Audience: What about a situation where you are caught in a relationship which feels completely wrong, which is destructive and hell-bent? Where it feels as if you are destroying each other? I can recognise very clearly the whole wounded, wounder, healer triangle in my own life.

Clare: Well, we would need to look at this much more closely, to see what is actually going on in your chart and whether Chiron is involved. As astrologers we are not in the business of trying to fix problems. If we were, then we would ourselves be trapped in a negative Chiron scenario of trying to force a solution. However, a careful analysis of the birth chart will help us to identify what is going on and just making something conscious can make a difference.

Audience: I have heard that Chiron either rules Sagittarius or Virgo?

Clare: Either of these may be right, but personally I prefer to keep the jury out on this question. I think it is important not to try to own or possess Chiron by anchoring it into the zodiac. This may also be a way of trying to 'fix it', which is probably not appropriate to the symbolism of Chiron as an outsider.

Chiron Aspects
Sally has Chiron in aspect to the Moon, Mercury, Mars and Saturn. This is a complex combination which will help us understand something about Sally's wounded animal nature, where, for so long as she is operating from a position of ego control, she will continue to feel vulnerable and therefore defensive. The **Chiron-Moon** contact indicates that Sally will be extremely sensitive to issues around mothering and nurturing. She may feel that, on some level, she was rejected by her own mother and may spend years searching for someone who will care for her and nurture her and make her feel safe. Equally, she may try to 'fix it' for her mother, who she is likely to see as needing her help and support. The **Chiron-Mercury** aspect indicates that Sally is likely to rely on her mental powers and on analytical thinking, rather than her instincts, in order to resolve any problems or difficulties.

With **Chiron-Mars**, Sally is likely to develop a kind of false strength and independence to enable her to function in the world, and may become overly aggressive and defensive if she senses that anyone is getting close to penetrating her defences. **Chiron-Saturn** is likely to be experienced as a fundamental lack of safety and containment, which is also indicated by the Moon-Chiron aspect. She is likely to try and fix this by developing a kind of rigid self sufficiency and sense of responsibility for and duty to others.

These aspects indicate where Sally needs to let go, develop self acceptance and devote herself to the teaching or healing or guidance of others. With so many Chiron contacts, Sally's true vocation may well be shamanic. She has much to give, but for so long as she tries to fix everything by being in control and remaining fiercely defended, she will not succeed. It is almost as if her life were intended for a different purpose than the one she is identified with. If she can come to terms with this and surrender her own neediness and defensiveness, and learn to trust her deep instinctive wisdom, she will be able to devote herself to others and focus her attention away from her own pain and woundedness.

David has Chiron in aspect to Mercury and Venus. How would you describe a **Chiron-Venus** contact?

Audience: Could this indicate a basic lack of self worth, a sense of not deserving to be loved or appreciated? If David is trying to 'fix' this, he is likely to do anything to gain other people's approval, which will only make it worse so that he will continue to drive people away?

Clare: Absolutely. However, if he can eventually learn to accept himself just as he is, then he will be able to value himself and others regardless of how awkward or flawed they may appear to be from a conventional point of view. The same can be said of his Chiron-Mercury contact. His own ideas and views and ways of communicating may not conform to general expectations, but if he can listen to his instincts, he will learn to speak his own truth and be able to help others do the same.

Notes
1. N. Campion, *The Great Year*, p.131.
2. C. G. Jung, *Psychology and Religion* CW11, p.25.
3. Richard Tarnas, *Prometheus the Awakener*.
4. J. M. Roberts, *A History of the World*.
5. Melanie Reinhart, *Chiron and the Healing Journey* and *To the Edge and Beyond*.

LESSON 6

Introduction to the Signs of the Zodiac

Each one of us is unique – we have our own individual way of seeing ourselves, of perceiving the world, and of reacting to particular circumstances. And yet, in spite of this uniqueness, there are also recognisable and predictable patterns within the human psyche. The fascination of astrology is that, once we have an individual's birth chart in front of us, we can assess how that particular individual is likely to react to certain situations.

An example of this which I often use is to imagine twelve people – each representing one of the twelve signs of the zodiac – waiting at a bus stop. They are on their way to work but the bus is late. How does each of these signs react? Obviously, the descriptions below are only caricatures, since nobody is a pure representation of only one sign, but the fact that these caricatures are so often recognisable illustrates the fact that the human beings conform to certain inherent patterns which we all share to some extent. To begin with, there are only likely to be ten people in this bus queue, because Aries and Sagittarius are likely to be missing.

Aries has probably never waited for a bus in his life. He simply can't bear to wait or to be dependent on other people or on situations outside his control. He needs to be in the driving seat himself. He has a set of rollerblades, a bicycle, motorbike or fast car to take him wherever he wants, whenever he needs, so that he can be independent and free to act instantaneously.

Taurus is realistic, practical and normally placid. He knows that everything takes time and that the bus will eventually arrive. He has a remarkable ability to live in the present. There is no point getting stressed or worried. After all, it is a beautiful day – the sun is shining, the grass is green, the trees are in their full bloom, the flowers in the nearby park are blooming and their smell fills the air. Life is good, as he breathes deeply, taking it all in.

Gemini is flexible and adaptable. He can use the extra time to do those hundred things that need catching up with. Using his mobile phone, he telephones work to let them know he will be late, speaks to his work colleague about his diary and meetings and makes alternative plans. While he is about it, he phones a friend to make plans to see the latest film that night, catches up by phoning his mother back, rings his sister/brother for a chat, makes changes to his diary, and finally takes out one of the two books or magazines he always carries with him for situations like this.

Cancer, on the other hand, feels personally let down, and can be thrown into despair and a curious depression by the late arrival of the bus. Retreating into his shell, he remembers clearly what it felt like in his childhood when his mother was late picking him up from school. His stomach churns at the memory, and he can feel clearly the feeling of abandonment as he waited, all alone, in the deserted playground at the end of the school day. How typical it is that, when he is always there for other people, he can't rely on anyone else being there for him.

For **Leo**, on the other hand, this is an unexpected opportunity to gather an audience – a crowd of admirers whom he seeks to entertain with some kind of drama or performance.

Virgo is becoming increasingly anxious and has noticed that his blood pressure is rising. Delving into his organiser-briefcase, he extracts the stress pills from one pocket and the digestion pills from another. All the jobs he had set himself for the day have been thrown into chaos and, like Gemini, he phones the office to reorganise things, trying to keep the rising panic and tension out of his voice.

Libra springs into action and tries to calm Virgo down with reassurances and logical thinking, explaining that nobody will blame Virgo for being late since it is not his fault.

Meanwhile, **Scorpio** is planning what to do to the bus driver when the bus finally arrives. Under his calm exterior, Scorpio is an unexploded bomb which, if the other people in the bus queue are lucky, will not go off. Nevertheless, at some point this will inevitably be detonated, possibly later in the day towards an unsuspecting work colleague.

Like Aries, **Sagittarius** is also absent from the bus queue. It is possible that he jogs to work, in order to use up some of the enormous physical energy which is a feature of this sign. Alternatively, Sagittarius is just as likely to travel to work by chauffeur driven limousine, or has hailed a passing cab – and to hell with the expense.

Capricorn waits with a grim sense of satisfaction and validation. He knew the bus would be late, since it validates his world view that everyone else is incompetent and irresponsible. He decides that the bus driver must have been late in turning up for duty and, because he is head of department at his work, he also decides to do a survey of his subordinates' arrival at work to see how much time is being wasted by the employees by this kind of irresponsibility.

Aquarius sees this late arrival as an opportunity to plan how the public transport system could be restructured. There must be a better way of managing this system, to enable ordinary people to get to work and contribute to the greater needs of society.

Pisces hasn't noticed that the bus is late, because he has drifted off into a world of his own.

Although these are, of course, gross caricatures of the signs, it may be that you can recognise the themes either in yourself or in people you know?

What is also interesting is the way we react to each other and how easy it is to blame or judge people for not responding to situations in the same way that we do. For example, Taurus may have no idea why Virgo is so tense and consider this to be a complete waste of energy to no effect. Gemini has no idea why Cancer has become so emotional since, after all, the lateness of the bus has provided several opportunities to catch up on bits and pieces, which would not otherwise have presented themselves. Libra, who doesn't know what he feels about the situation personally, will do whatever he can to calm the situation for everyone else, since that will make him feel much better. Capricorn doesn't know why Leo is showing off so much, this kind of behaviour is unnecessarily attention seeking and childish. Aquarius blames Taurus for taking the situation so philosophically – only by being public spirited and joining the cause for better public transport, can the situation be improved.

The Zodiac in Time

I want to introduce you to the signs of the zodiac in terms of the annual cycle of the Sun which defines the seasons in the northern hemisphere. Since our western astrology originates in the northern hemisphere, the astrological year is born in the spring, reaches the height of its strength

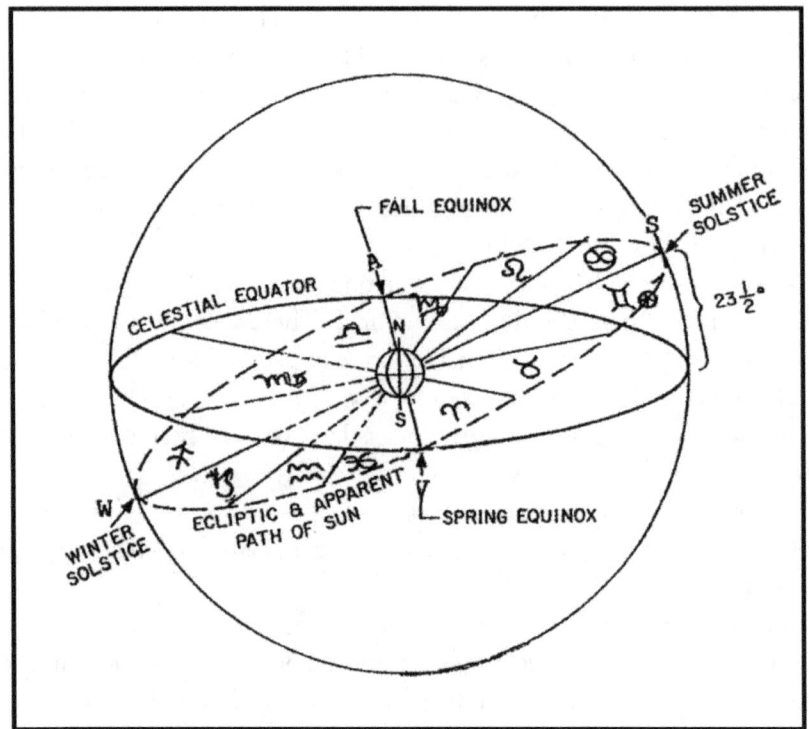

The signs of the zodiac[1]

and light in the summer, moves on to autumn and falls back to its darkest and weakest in the winter before being reborn once again the following spring.

The Signs of the Zodiac
Astrology is a geocentric system, with the Earth at the centre of the celestial sphere. The Earth's equator is projected onto the celestial sphere as the celestial equator. The path of the Sun, called the Ecliptic, is at an angle of 23.5° to the celestial equator, and it is this angle which creates the seasons. The Ecliptic is divided into twelve equal zodiac signs of 30° each, and the Sun spends approximately one month in each of these signs as it moves around the Ecliptic each year.

There are four cardinal points in the year: two equinoxes and two solstices. The spring or vernal equinox ('equinox' means equal night and day) each year marks the Sun's entrance into the sign of Aries, the first sign of the zodiac. At this time of year, normally around 21st March, the Sun crosses the equator and enters the northern hemisphere. For the next three months, the Sun continues its northward journey, rising higher and higher in the sky as it enters the sign of Taurus (approximately 21st April) and Gemini (approximately 21st May). The days get longer and progressively warmer.

The summer solstice each year marks the date (normally 21st June) when the Sun reaches its highest point in the northern hemisphere (on the Tropic of Cancer, which is 23.5° degrees north of the equator) and appears to 'stand still' (the meaning of 'solstice') before beginning its southward journey. On this date the Sun enters the sign of Cancer. For the next three months, the Sun will lose height in the northern hemisphere, entering the sign of Leo (approximately 23rd July) and Virgo (approximately 23rd August). The year matures, the days are hot and increasingly dry.

The autumn equinox each year marks the Sun's entrance into the sign of Libra. At this time of year, normally around 21st September, the Sun crosses the equator and enters the southern hemisphere. For the next three months, the Sun continues to lose height as it enters the sign of Scorpio (approximately 23rd October) and Sagittarius (approximately 23rd November). The days begin to get shorter and colder.

The winter solstice each year marks the date (normally 22nd December) when the Sun reaches its most southerly point (on the Tropic of Capricorn, 23.5° degrees south of the equator) and once again appears to 'stand still' for approximately three days before beginning its northward journey. On this date the Sun enters the sign of Capricorn. For the next three months, the days begin to get longer again as the Sun travels northwards, entering the sign of Aquarius (approximately 21st January) and Pisces (21st February) until once again it crosses the equator at the spring equinox.

The following table shows the approximate dates of the Sun's entrance into the astrological signs. These dates vary by a day or so from year to year, so it is always worth checking the year in question to find out the exact date and time when the Sun enters any of the signs.

The Seasonal Year

Approximate Date	Cardinal Point	Sun enters:	Sign	Mode
21 March	Spring Equinox	Aries	♈	Cardinal
21 April		Taurus	♉	Fixed
21 May		Gemini	♊	Mutable
21 June	Summer Solstice	Cancer	♋	Cardinal
23 July		Leo	♌	Fixed
23 August		Virgo	♍	Mutable
23 September	Autumn Equinox	Libra	♎	Cardinal
23 October		Scorpio	♏	Fixed
23 November		Sagittarius	♐	Mutable
22 December	Winter Solstice	Capricorn	♑	Cardinal
21 January		Aquarius	♒	Fixed
21 February		Pisces	♓	Mutable

As you can see from the above, the two solstices and two equinoxes mark the beginning of the four cardinal signs – which are followed by the fixed signs which in turn are followed by the mutable signs.

The Symbols for the Zodiac Signs

The origin of the symbols for the zodiac signs appears to be lost in history. Some of the symbols appear in Greek horoscopes which are about 2,000 years old, some of them seem to be alchemical signs, and some of them relate to the shape of the constellations themselves.

Introduction to the Signs of the Zodiac

Aries the Ram

The symbol for Aries can be described as resembling the face and horns of a goat or ram, or the eyebrows and nose of the face, which are said to be prominent in Aries people. Alternatively this symbol is similar to that of a plant shoot when it first emerges from the ground in the spring.

Taurus the Bull

The symbol for Taurus has been described as the head of a bull, again with horns. It has also been described as the Moon resting on the Sun. Compared with the symbol for Aries, it has a nice solid round shape.

Gemini the Twins

Gemini's symbol is based on the twin stars Castor and Pollux in the constellation of Gemini. It is literally the Roman numeral II, and the theme of duality is the key to the meaning of this sign.

Cancer the Crab

The symbol for Cancer is circular, internal and protective. It has been described as symbolising the ovaries, the breasts and to the closeness of the mother/child relationship, reflecting the nurturing quality of this sign.

Leo the Lion

The symbol for Leo is similar to the stars in the constellation of Leo. It has also been described as the head and mane of a lion.

Virgo the Virgin

See the description for Scorpio, below.

Libra the Scales

The sign of Libra was a later addition to the zodiac, being placed between the signs of Virgo and Scorpio, 'borrowing' the claws of Scorpio to form the scales of Libra. It has been described as a dairy maid's yoke, used to balance two pails of milk. It has also been described as a symbol of the Sun setting over the western horizon, since Libra is also associated with the western side of the horoscope.

Scorpio the Scorpion   ♏

The symbols for Virgo and Scorpio are remarkably similar, since they are both created from an identical 'm' – an ancient medical symbol. Both Virgo and Scorpio are associated with medicine and healing. The two constellations of Virgo and Scorpio are extremely large and easily identifiable in the night sky. The enclosed shape in the symbol for Virgo and the 'sting' in the scorpion's tail have been described as the feminine and masculine versions of the same symbol.

Sagittarius the Archer   ♐

The glyph for Sagittarius is also similar to the constellation, with the archer's arrow pointing upwards ready to be shot into the sky. The line across the arrow is said to symbolise the fact that Sagittarius is a centaur, half human and half horse.

Capricorn the Goat   ♑

The symbol for Capricorn contains the v-shape of the goat's head and the fish tale of the sea goat, since the constellation of Capricorn is found in the 'southern seas' of the celestial sphere. Alternatively, it has also been described as the goat bending down on its knees.

Aquarius the Water Bearer   ♒

The symbol for Aquarius describes air waves or radio waves and particularly relates to the travelling of information through the air.

Pisces the Fish   ♓

Pisces is the symbol of two fish or dolphins yoked together.

Zodiac Signs versus Constellations

It is worth knowing at this stage that the twelve zodiac **signs** are not the same thing as the twelve **constellations** (or star groups). As we have seen above, the signs of the zodiac are twelve equal 30° sections of the ecliptic, related to the seasonal year and anchored to the four cardinal points of the sun's annual journey. Western astrology, which is based on the seasonal year, uses the tropical or seasonal zodiac. Indian or vedic astrology uses the sidereal (or 'star') zodiac, based on the positions of the stars in the actual constellations, which are star groups of very different sizes. Owing to a phenomenon caused by the earth's 'wobble' on its axis, the two zodiacs have gradually, over the last two thousand years or so, started to drift out of alignment with each other.

Audience: Can you say more about this? I'm not sure that I understand.

Clare: Perhaps the best way to imagine this is as two concentric circles, the outer circle representing the backdrop of the stars, containing the twelve constellations, and the inner circle divided into the twelve signs of the zodiac, each 30 degrees in length. Approximately 2,000 years ago these two circles lined up, with the beginning of the constellation of Aries and the beginning of the zodiac sign of Aries in the same place. Since that time, these two circles have been moving in opposite directions at the rate of one degree every 72 years. They will not line up again for approximately 26,000 years. This 26,000 year cycle has itself been divided into twelve 'astrological ages' of approximately 2,000 years each.

For the last 2,000 years, at the spring equinox, the Sun has in fact been rising against the constellation of Pisces and will gradually begin to rise against the constellation of Aquarius, heralding the start of the new astrological age referred to in the 1960s' musical *Hair* as the dawn of the Age of Aquarius. In another 2,000 years, when the Sun begins to rise against the constellation of Capricorn, we will enter a new Age of Capricorn, which doesn't have quite the same ring to it. The astrological ages have their own meanings too, although these are on a quite different scale. Western astrology uses the tropical zodiac as its primary frame of reference, and eastern, Indian, or vedic astrology uses the sidereal zodiac as its primary frame of reference. The difference between the two zodiacs is now approximately 26°.

Audience: Does that mean that my Sun could be in the previous sign in sidereal astrology?

Clare: Yes, if your Sun is between 0° and 25° of a sign. Rather than letting this bother us too much, I think we need to appreciate that every culture has its own sky lore and its own astrology, which is an expression of the history, mythology, religion and philosophy of the culture in which it has developed. As a broad generalisation, we can say that the western tropical zodiac is solar because we use a solar calendar. This reflects the emphasis in western cultures on self sufficiency, self expression and the development of the individual. The eastern sidereal zodiac on the other hand, belongs to cultures where the Moon is the basis of the calendar and of the annual festivals. Eastern astrology is not so focused on the development of the individual but puts the emphasis on community and family and tends to take a more fated approach than western psychological astrology. You will have experienced this for yourselves if you have ever had your chart done in India. It is a much more fated kind of astrology.

Planetary Rulers of the Signs
Each of the zodiac signs has a planetary ruler – a planet which is said to function strongly and be particularly comfortable and 'at home' in the sign. The planetary rulers of the signs were allocated by the Greeks in a symmetrical and balanced proportion, with each planet having rulership over two signs, one positive and one negative, except for the Sun and Moon, which each have rulership over only one sign. The planetary rulers are distributed evenly amongst the signs in order of their observed distance from the earth, as follows:

The Sun has rulership over the sign of Leo, the hottest time of the year when the Sun is at the height of its strength. The Moon has rulership over the sign of Cancer, which begins with the summer solstice, marking the Sun's change of direction. Moving outwards in decreasing orbital speeds, Mercury comes next, and has rulership over both the signs of Gemini and Virgo. Then comes Venus, ruling both the signs of Taurus and Libra, then Mars which rules Aries and Scorpio, then Jupiter which rules Pisces and Sagittarius. Finally, at the coldest and darkest time of the year, Saturn as the slowest planet, has rulership over the signs of Aquarius and Capricorn. The outer planets are relatively recent newcomers and have been added to this model: Pluto as the modern ruler of Scorpio, Uranus as the modern ruler of Aquarius and Neptune as the modern ruler of Pisces.

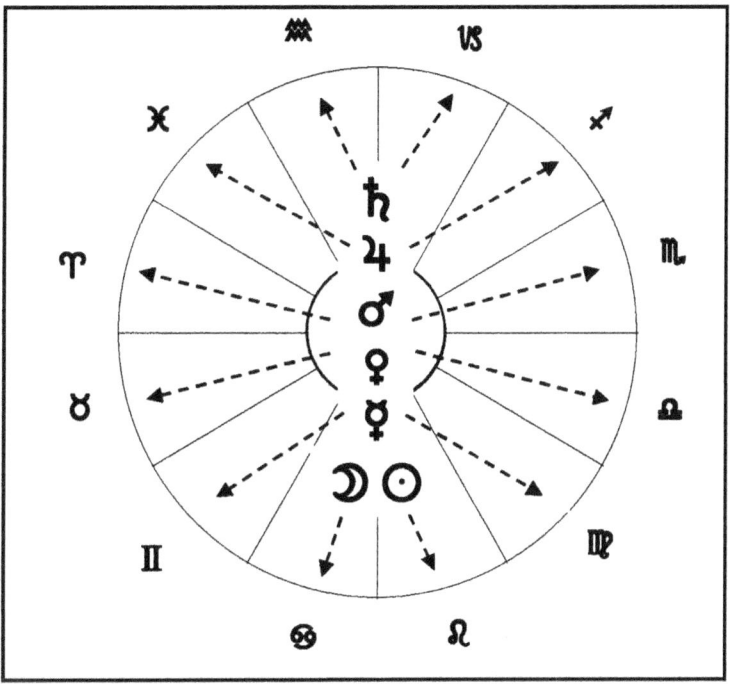

Planets in Exaltation, Detriment and Fall

In addition to the planetary rulerships, there are also planets which are exalted in the signs, which again means that they are comfortable and tend to function well in those signs. The table below indicates which planets are exalted in the various signs. Planets will be in detriment, however, in signs opposite the signs they rule. Planets in detriment are traditionally considered to have difficulty operating positively in these signs. Finally, in addition to planets in detriment, planets are also said to be in their fall in certain signs, which means that they are debilitated in those signs.

My own feeling is that this traditional system of rulerships, exaltations and debilities is extremely important for psychological astrology. It gives us valuable clues about which planets need particular care and attention, in order that they can be redeemed and positively integrated into our lives as we strive to balance the opposites within our own psyches. We will examine this in much greater detail when we study the meaning of each of the signs of the zodiac in turn, but for the time being, it is worth explaining briefly what I mean.

Sign	Ruler	Exalted	Detriment	Fall
Aries	Mars	Sun	Venus	Saturn
Taurus	Venus	Moon	Mars	
Gemini	Mercury		Jupiter	
Cancer	Moon	Jupiter	Saturn	Mars
Leo	Sun		Saturn	
Virgo	Mercury		Jupiter	
Libra	Venus	Saturn	Mars	Sun
Scorpio	Mars (Pluto)		Venus	Moon
Sagittarius	Jupiter		Mercury	
Capricorn	Saturn	Mars	Moon	Jupiter
Aquarius	Saturn (Uranus)		Sun	
Pisces	Jupiter (Neptune)	Venus	Mercury	

With the Sun in Aries, for example, an individual is unlikely to have difficulty expressing the qualities of Mars or the Sun, which will come naturally. The challenge for the Sun in Aries, however, will be the conscious integration of Venus and Saturn, traditionally in their detriment and fall in Aries, into their sense of identity. If this can be achieved, the Aries Sun person will have learned to value and to relate to others (Venus) and will have developed the self-discipline and patience (Saturn) to enable them to lead and to inspire others in a mature, measured and effective way, as a fully integrated Aries Sun individual.

Equally, with the Sun in Libra, the individual is unlikely to have difficulty expressing the qualities of Venus or Saturn. The challenge for the Sun in Libra, however, will be the conscious integration of the qualities of Mars and the Sun, which, from a psychological point of view, we could say is an essential part of the process of individuation. If this can be achieved, the Libra Sun individual will have found their metal (Mars) and be able to act with focus, courage and determination (Mars) for the greater good (Libra) and to fight (Mars) for what they value (Venus). As they develop personal courage, and become less dependent on the good opinions of others, the Libran will lose the vacillation and hesitation for which this sign is so well known, and become an authority (Sun) in issues of justice and fairness (Libra), prepared to take responsibility (Saturn) for the consequences of their actions (Libra), not unlike King Solomon himself.

Notes
1. Adapted from a diagram in: John Lash, *Quest for the Zodiac*.

LESSON 7

Constructing the Zodiac

Number Symbolism

> The symbolism of number enables us to devise a comprehensive and coherent interrelated system in which science, religion, art and philosophy define and explore specific aspects of the whole without ever losing sight of each other.[1]

We have already seen the symmetrical distribution of the planetary rulers of the zodiac signs, and the twelve-fold structure of the zodiac is a model of the universe (the macrocosm) and of each individual human being (the microcosm), which is also symmetrically balanced, harmonious and extraordinarily comprehensive. It is in this ordered symmetry that we can find the core meaning of each of the signs of the zodiac, and I want to describe to you how the zodiac is constructed in terms of the number symbolism, which runs right through astrology and without which astrology cannot be truly understood. Number symbolism provides the central clue not only to the interpretation of the astrological signs, but also to the understanding and interpretation of the planets, houses and aspects, as well as a host of other astrological techniques. It is the door and the key to the door into a true understanding of the astrological world of the psyche. As Jung discovered, number symbolism is not only fundamental to astrology and to alchemy, but can also be defined psychologically as an 'archetype of order which has become conscious'.[2]

Although the 360° circle and the twelve 30° divisions of the circle were originally devised by the Mesopotamian priest/astrologers from the second millennium BCE onwards, we owe the construction of the astrological chart as it is used today to the symbolic mathematics of the ancient Greek philosopher/mathematicians who, from the seventh century BCE, made leaps and bounds in the development of the science, art and craft of astrology. The ancient Greeks believed that truth was, by its very nature, good, harmonious and beautiful, and they created a symmetrical and well balanced model of the universe and of the horoscope which, for the first time, they started applying not only to leaders and kings, as personifications of their countries, but also to individual human beings. The immensely influential philosopher/mathematician, mystic and sage, Pythagoras, believed that numbers were qualities which described not only the nature of the universe but also the nature of any system, including the human being. The mathematical model devised by Pythagoras is known as the tetractys, one of the most deceptively simple and yet profound models that exists in the western tradition. The tetractys is a rich, many-layered symbol with a rich flow of meanings, relationships and correspondences. Simply expressed, the Pythagoreans believed that the nature of all things could be understood and described according to the powers of the one, the two, the three and the four as an unfolding sequence of creation. These numbers are not simply quantitative, but they are also archetypes of number, with 'oneness', 'twoness', 'threeness' and 'fourness' being understood as wholes or unities in themselves, each with their own qualitative meaning.

Number as an Archetype of Cosmic Order

Horoscope structure		Astrological aspects
Unity: The whole chart	◯	Conjunction ☌
Polarity: Positive/Negative	◯ ◯	Opposition ☍
Three Modes: Cardinal/Fixed/Mutable	◯ ◯ ◯	Trine △
Four Elements: Earth/Air/Fire/Water	◯ ◯ ◯ ◯	Square □

The Tetractys: $1 + 2 + 3 + 4 = 10^3$

The astrological chart is an exact representation of the tetractys, being itself a unity, with each of the twelve signs of the zodiac being simultaneously polar (active or passive), modal (cardinal, fixed or mutable) and elemental (fire, earth, air, water). The number twelve is a remarkably complete number in which the polarity is repeated six times, the modes are repeated four times and the elements are repeated three times.

The Tetractys as a Developmental Model

The tetractys provides a useful model for the process of psychological development which is remarkably similar to the various stages or processes recognised by the alchemists. Broadly speaking, the task is twofold. The initial task is to identify and differentiate each of the different levels since, as the alchemists repeatedly stated, 'only separated things can unite'. Once the process of separation and differentiation has been achieved, the remaining task is to integrate all the different levels into a conscious unity and wholeness.

Polarity

> That which is made up of both the opposites is one, and when this one is dissected the opposites appear.[4]

> All things are double, one against another.[5]

Polarity emerges out of the original unity in what is called the 'primal schism', or the 'separation of the world parents'. The creation myths of almost every culture describe the first division out of the primordial ocean, or chaos, which creates by dividing itself, in the same way that a living cell divides and becomes two. Everything in time and space is governed by the opposites and swings between them. Opposites both repel and attract each other; they are fundamentally united because they share the same source, which is the original unity. Even our language reflects this split, with many words beginning with the prefix 'di-' describing the separation of something which has previously been whole, or one. For example: di-vide, di-scern, di-sect, di-stinguish, di-vorce, di-chotomy and so on.

The 'problem of opposites' has always been a subject of fascination in many different fields of study, such as mysticism, philosophy, mathematics, science and psychology. The Gurdjieff scholar Maurice Nicoll observes that 'Opposites are inseparable, and although one is against the other, you cannot have one without the other, any more than you can have a stick with only one end.'[6] In other words, darkness implies light and light darkness. They are mutually destructive and yet neither can exist without the other. The law of opposites keeps everything in balance since, taken to extremes, they become one another. For example, taken to extremes, east becomes west, day becomes night, love becomes hate, attraction becomes repulsion, and so on.

In psychology, the law of opposites helps us to understand how people process information and function in the world. The psychotherapist Martin Buber described his experience of polarity as follows:

> In my experience, if I come near to the reality of a person, I experience it as a polar reality. I would say now that when I grasp him more broadly and more deeply than before, I see his whole polarity and then I see how the worst in him and the best in him are dependent on one another, attached to one another. And this polarity is very often directionless. It is a chaotic state. We could bring a cosmic note into it. We can help – we may be able to help him just by helping him to change the relation between the poles. We can put order, put a shape into this.[7]

This same idea is found in psychosynthesis: 'People identified with one pole may be rich in the quality of the opposite one, but repress it, and consciously devalue it.'[8]

Polarity as the Basis of Psychological Projection
The psychic mechanism of projection is one of the most important ideas in psychology and in psychological astrology. This means that whenever we identify consciously with one end of a polarity, the opposite end will become unconscious and be projected onto other people or onto the world, from where it will operate in a compensatory fashion. In other words, we will be constantly confronted by our unknown opposites, not realising that they belong to us. Whenever we are attracted toward a desired object, or repelled away from a hated object, we are caught up in the drama of the opposites. As Jung observed, what we cannot accept about ourselves comes back to us as fate. Astrologically, this duality is found alternately in the twelve signs of the zodiac, six of which are positive, masculine or yang, and six of which are negative, feminine, or yin in their orientation. Each of the signs, therefore, reflects the fundamental polarities which exist within the manifest world and within the individual. This is also the core meaning of the astrological aspect of the opposition.

The positive or, in Chinese philosophy, yang principle describes motion from a centre outwards. A yang orientation is a driving energy, forceful, active, impulsive and dominant. It creates and destroys. The positive signs describe object-oriented, sociable people who are not afraid to jump into unknown situations. The negative or yin principle is subject-oriented, receptive, yielding, enclosing, withdrawing and inward moving. The yin individual 'is characterised by a reflective nature which causes him always to think and consider before acting. His shyness and distrust of things induces hesitation, and so he always has difficulty in adapting to the external world'.[9] Jung recognised the inherent polarity within the human psyche as 'extroversion' and 'introversion', terms which are now so widely recognised that they become part of our ordinary vocabulary. As Whitmont[10] observes, the introvert has object fear, instinctively pulling away from the external world. The extrovert, on the other hand, has subject fear, undervaluing and mistrusting his inner world.

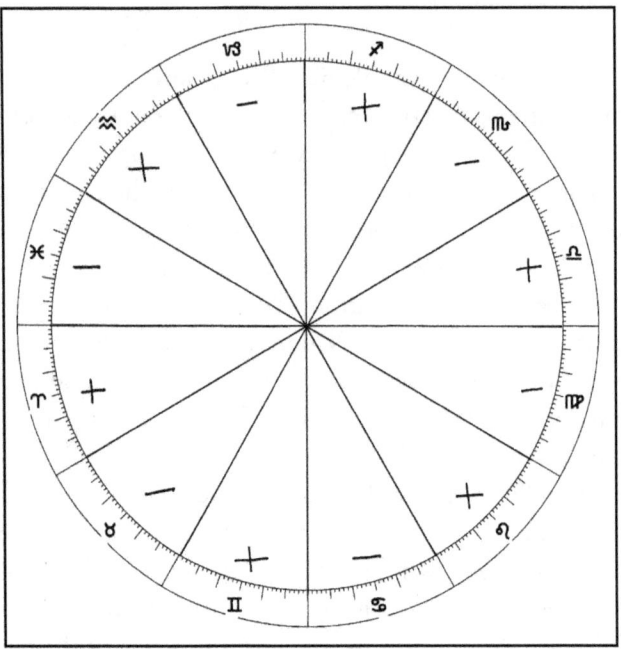

POSITIVE: Acting, Doing, Yang energy		NEGATIVE: Passive, Being, Yin energy	
Aries	♈	Taurus	♉
Gemini	♊	Cancer	♋
Leo	♌	Virgo	♍
Libra	♎	Scorpio	♏
Sagittarius	♐	Capricorn	♑
Aquarius	♒	Pisces	♓

Now let's have a look at your own birth charts. It will be interesting and revealing to discover who are the extroverts here and who are the introverts.

Audience: How do you find out?

Clare: First, identify the seven planets: Sun, Moon, Mercury, Venus and Mars, Jupiter, Saturn and count how many fall in positive signs and how many fall in negative signs. For the purposes of this exercise, ignore the positions of the outer planets – Uranus, Neptune and Pluto – the Node and Chiron for two reasons. Firstly, although these points provide information about the collective and generational background into which we are born, they won't tell us anything about our own unique personal orientation. Secondly, they each describe a particular kind of challenge or struggle, and should not therefore be considered as plus points in terms of assessing polarity balance.

Have a look at our two example charts. You can see that David has four planets in positive signs (Sun and Jupiter in Aries, Mars in Leo and Saturn in Aquarius) and three planets in negative signs (Mercury in Taurus, Moon in Capricorn and Venus in Pisces). Sally, on the other hand, has five planets in positive signs (Jupiter in Gemini, Saturn in Leo, Mercury, Sun and Venus in Aquarius) and only two in negative signs (Mars in Cancer, and Moon in Pisces). This tells us that David has a natural balance between positive and negative, masculine and feminine. He has the potential to consciously integrate both poles within himself and the ability to move gracefully and rhythmically between opposites. Sally has a more outward going, extravert nature, which means that she is naturally object-oriented, and will derive her meaning and sense of purpose from actively engaging with the outside world. The question is whether she is actually living this out in her life. Although her birth chart tells us one thing, her parental and social conditioning may have led her to suppress this aspect of her nature.

Audience: So although her chart is yang in nature she may not be living this out in her life?

Clare: That's right, and this is a good example of how astrology can help us to become more who we really are in essence. It is perfectly possible that Sally has received many messages in her life that she should hold back, be more 'feminine', sensitive and accommodating, and she may well have adapted herself to the expectations of others, which is something we all do to some extent. Once she learns that her birth chart shows a natural positive orientation, then she can start to give herself permission to become more who she is in essence, which can feel like a powerful release.

But the law of opposites is never that straightforward because, as Sally develops her natural yang orientation, the opposite end of the spectrum is likely to become unconscious and be projected onto other people or onto the world. This means that she will find herself in situations where she is required to reflect and withdraw and to put the needs of others first. From a conscious yang standpoint, this can be extremely frustrating, but it is simply an example of the way that psychic opposites both challenge and complete each other. So we could say that, as Sally develops her natural yang orientation, it is important that she doesn't lose touch with, or project onto others, her own much more sensitive Mars and Moon, which are in negative signs.

Audience: I have a count of four positive and three negative signs.

Clare: Most of us will have a relatively equal balance of planets in the positive and negative signs. This tells us that, on this level at least, there is nothing that needs to be particularly noted when we are preparing to interpret a chart. There is a potential balance between the opposite orientations.

Has anyone found a marked emphasis? Who is significantly 'yin' in orientation? This will be the case if you have at least two more points in negative signs than in positive signs. So there are four of you who are significantly yin. Now that you have discovered this, it could well be quite a relief. This gives you permission to be more introverted, to pay attention to your own inner world, to stay at home and read a book, listen to music, write your journal or watch a film, rather than force yourself to go out to a party or feel guilty because you are not involved in any political or social causes?

Audience: (Male) I have five planets in negative signs and two in positive signs. I have never really thought of myself as an introvert.

Clare: Well, perhaps this is something to think about? It can be enormously validating to discover our true personal orientation and even such a simple discovery as this, right at the beginning of our astrological studies, can give us permission to become more 'who we are in essence', rather than to try and distort ourselves into being what others, or what society expects us to be.

Audience: (Female) In my chart Mars is the only planet in a positive sign, and I think that what people see is my Mars, but actually I am very 'yin' by nature.

Clare: This sounds like a good example of projection. Your natural orientation is private and introverted, but it seems that you meet your own Mars in projection, in the form of other people or in your dealings with the outside world, such as in your career and in other outer challenges. My suggestion is that it would be worth getting to know your Mars a bit better, so that it can serve you, help you achieve your goals and to assert and defend yourself if necessary, rather than simply meeting it 'out there'.

Audience: So people who are mostly introverted attract extroverts, and people who are mostly extroverted attract introverts? What you don't have inside you attract from the outside world?

Clare: Exactly. What we have in our birth charts is already ours – we live with it all the time, we know it and it belongs to us. We don't need to attract any more of it from the outside world because we have enough of our own. Another way of saying this is that the polarity which is lacking or absent in our birth charts is unknown to our conscious minds or is missing from our social adaptation, and is therefore projected onto others who express that particular polarity strongly. This is why opposites both attract and repel us in equal measure.

Audience: (Female) I have six planets in yang signs.

Clare: So this means that you naturally draw your meaning and energy from the outside world, from activity and involvement and achievements in the world and from your involvement with the community at large.

Audience: That's true, but I always find myself being challenged, which makes me very uncomfortable because I don't like to be seen as the dominant female in a room – I get very angry with myself, because I don't like being seen to be aggressive – it makes me feel like a man. And I have difficulty finding a man who is strong enough for me.

Clare: It is interesting that you have used the words 'challenge', 'dominant', 'aggressive', 'angry' and 'strong' – which are all very yang words, describing a competitive, masculine orientation. It is not uncommon for women with predominantly yang charts to feel uncomfortable about being too powerful, or to be concerned about finding a partner who is strong enough for them. Your capacity to function effectively in the world and to stand up for yourself is not in doubt. Your major underlying concern, however, seems to be driven by the opposite yin pole, because it is about finding a partner who will complete you, reflect you and support you. It may be that you will feel more balanced, completed and whole in a relationship with a man who is predominantly yin, and therefore not in competition with you. Do you see what I mean?

Audience: Well, it is certainly true that most of my friends are yin, and it is extraordinary how I always seem to attract these kinds of people. I can be just sitting on a bus and suddenly the person next to me is telling me their life story. And then I find myself trying to fix other people's problems. For example, if someone comes along and sobs 'someone has just died' or 'I've lost my house', then I want to fix it, and I know that this is a very masculine characteristic. What really annoys me is that they just want to wallow in it, so why are they telling me? And then I feel bad because I seem to be unkind. The other thing is that I am the eldest child in my family and my mother is very yin – flaky and frail – but actually she is a great deal stronger in reality. I have noticed that yin people often seem frail but are actually much stronger than yang people.

Clare: Yes, I think that is because, although yang people are generally very strong in the world, they haven't necessarily developed the inner resources to fall back on. Yin people, on the other hand, have a deep inner reservoir to draw from when necessary. In a crisis the yin people get very strong.

Audience: That's right. We have fallen apart, but they are able to cope.

Audience: I am struggling a bit with these ideas, because if you are saying that yin attracts yang and yang attracts yin, then it seems that you are also saying that everything means everything, in which case it all becomes meaningless?

Clare: I can understand exactly what you are saying, and it is an important point. Although these differences are very powerful, they are also subtle because they define fundamentally different orientations which nevertheless complement and complete each other. It can take a while for this to fall into place, particularly if both psychological ideas and astrology are new to us. However, as our astrological knowledge develops, we meet this same idea again and again until it begins to make sense. I could have taken a different approach and presented this to you in a much simpler way. I could be describing an extrovert as someone with a predominance of planets in positive signs, and an introvert as someone with a predominance of planets in negative signs. This would be much easier to grasp, but it is not the whole story and nor is it a true reflection of our experience. So I am trying to introduce you to the psychological complexity of it right at the beginning.

Astrology is the only model I have come across which sufficiently reflects the subtle complexities of the human condition, and there are times when we all have to suspend disbelief as we pick it all to pieces, until we can begin to see the whole picture, at which point we can start putting it all back together again. I don't know the answer except to say that it is worth persevering and to question all the time. Your observation is very important and I suggest that you hang on to the scepticism.

Audience: Oh no, I won't hang on. I need to be more open-minded.

Notes
1. John Anthony West, *Serpent in the Sky: The High Wisdom of Ancient Egypt* (1979), p.65.
2. C.G. Jung, *Synchronicity: An Acausal Connecting Principle*, CW 8 para 816–968.
3. Adapted from a diagram entitled 'The process of psychological development' in Edinger, E.F., *The Mysterium Lectures*, p.279.
4. Philo – Alexandrian school, first century AD.
5. *Ecclesiasticus* (XLII 24).
6. Maurice Nicoll, *Psychological Commentaries on the Teaching of Gurdjieff & Ouspensky*, Volume One, p.320.
7. In Carl Rogers *Dialogues*, Kirschenbaum & Henderson (eds) See also: Martin Buber, *I and Thou*.
8. Pierro Ferrucci, *What We May Be*.
9. Edward C. Whitmont, *The Symbolic Quest*, p.139–40.
10. Ibid.

LESSON 8

Modes and Elements

Modes: Cardinal, Fixed and Mutable Signs

Symbolically, the number three refers to the establishment of a relationship between two previously unrelated or opposing principles. For example, a line drawn between two points creates a relationship between these two points. What is particularly relevant about the symbolic nature of the number three is that our logical, discriminating minds have difficulty understanding it, because the intellect is divisive and polar by nature. 'Understanding' is an emotional, rather than an intellectual, function. It comes from the heart rather than the head. We could say that the number three is a quality of the soul rather than of the spirit. The more we understand, the more we are able to reconcile and relate. For example, words beginning with the prefix 're-' (which literally means 'back again') tend to be gentle, healing words describing the bringing together of what has been previously separated: re-member, re-lationship, re-medy, re-pair, re-solve, re-form, re-concile, re-cognise, etc. The number three teaches us that true and false are relative and that some kind of equilibrium between positive and negative forces is possible, such as occur, for example, in the forces of action, reaction and equilibrium. The Greek philosophers used the system of thesis, antithesis and synthesis in their rhetoric, and three exists in Chinese philosophy as the yin, the yang and the tao, which is the middle road between opposites.

The law of three can be observed in action in very many different areas of life. In sport, for example, where there are two opposing teams, the referee or umpire is the third force whose job it is to mediate between the two sides and to keep the game moving forwards without war breaking out. Or in a court of law, where the judge is the third force overseeing and mediating between the prosecution and defence counsels, or in the British House of Commons, where the two opposing political parties face each other in debate and are mediated by the Speaker of the House.

Without this third force there is no possibility of a creative resolution, since each side would be endlessly trying to conquer and destroy the other.

When we are caught at the either/or level of duality or polarity, then we can be paralysed by a sterile, static, rigid kind of indecision in which we find ourselves weighing up the opposites, identifying first with one end and then with the other, but without being able to find a relationship between them. Jung's advice in situations of this sort is for the individual to first make both ends of the spectrum fully conscious and to deliberately suffer the tension of the opposites, since 'every tension of opposites culminates in a release out of which comes the third and in the third the tension is resolved and the lost unity is restored'.[1] This is a very profound idea and extremely helpful to live by, once we have grasped it.

Audience: Do you mean to say that solutions can't be worked out using reason or logic?

Clare: Yes. Although the use of reason and logic is an essential part of the process of identifying the alternative options and choices and the consequences of either choice, the intellect alone cannot provide the solution. If we are fortunate, and have the faith to be able to sit with the tension of uncertainty and indecision, an inclusive resolution, which does not deny either end of the spectrum but includes both, will emerge from somewhere other than the intellect. This is the third force. We could even describe this as the wisdom of the soul, which has long been considered to have three parts. It is said that Plato adopted his doctrine of the tripartite soul from the Pythagoreans. For Plato, one part is 'spirited' [cardinal], another part 'desires the pleasures of nutrition and generation' [fixed] and the last part is 'reasoning' [mutable]. When each part receives what it is due, the soul is brought into a state of harmony.

Audience: My daughter has Sun in Libra, and she is very rational and skilful at balancing up ideas until she is completely paralysed and doesn't know what to do. It's funny that you say this because I have started suggesting to her that she sleeps on the problem to see if a solution presents itself to her. Otherwise, we get into a 26 hour discussion about either/or which never helps, and ends up making both of us miserable.

Audience: This is an interesting idea, but either way seems to involve suffering?

Clare: That is true. The alternative is to identify solely with one end of the spectrum. This certainly reduces the tension on a superficial level, but is a move away from our task of differentiation and integration, and will not help us to tend to the soul's need for balance and harmony.

Cardinal, Fixed and Mutable Signs

In astrology, the three forces, or modes, are known as cardinal, fixed and mutable; or initiating, resisting and mediating/accommodating. In exactly the same way, when the birth chart is divided into three, the 120 degree aspect known as the trine describes relationship, resolution and harmony. If we consider the first three signs of the zodiac, the primal force is Aries – cardinal Fire, followed by the equally powerful resistance of the second sign of Taurus – fixed Earth, creating a polarity which is only resolved by the third sign of Gemini – mutable Air, with its ability to relate, communicate and to mediate between the two opposing forces without taking sides. This same theme is repeated around the zodiac, with cardinal energy followed by fixed energy and resolved by mutable energy, whether this is Cancer, Leo and Virgo; Libra, Scorpio and Sagittarius, or Capricorn, Aquarius and Pisces.

Each sign of the zodiac is either cardinal, fixed or mutable. You can see from this diagram that we can now add the modes to the polarities, which gives us another level of information with which to understand the meaning of the zodiac signs. We have already identified the signs according to their polarity, and the modes describe an additional level of orientation and motivation. The motivation of the cardinal signs of Aries, Cancer, Libra and Capricorn is to initiate and to achieve. The motivation of the fixed signs of Taurus, Leo, Scorpio and Aquarius is to resist and stabilise, and the motivation of the mutable signs of Gemini, Virgo, Sagittarius and Pisces is to adapt, mediate and reconcile.

Audience: So, are you saying that the mutable signs reflect the meaning of the number three?

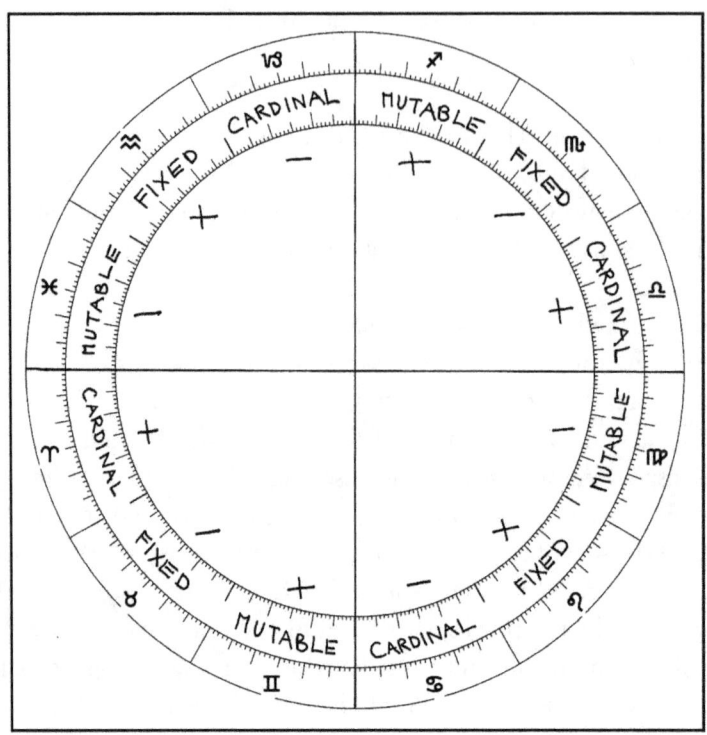

CARDINAL: Initiating, goal oriented

| Aries | ♈ | Cancer | ♋ |
| Libra | ♎ | Capricorn | ♑ |

FIXED: Steadfast, loyal, stable

| Taurus | ♉ | Leo | ♌ |
| Scorpio | ♏ | Aquarius | ♒ |

MUTABLE: Adaptable, flexible

| Gemini | ♊ | Virgo | ♍ |
| Sagittarius | ♐ | Pisces | ♓ |

Clare: Yes, they are the reconciling signs. The mutable signs do not really have their own clear motivation, other than to remain fluid and flexible. This is why they are so good at mediating between the 'unstoppable force' of the cardinal signs and the 'immovable object' of the fixed signs. Mutable signs are adaptable, adjustable, changeable, flexible and restless.

The cardinal signs of Aries, Cancer, Libra and Capricorn are initiating and goal-oriented. Cardinal people start ventures, they have a vision of what has to be achieved, they are self-motivated. They challenge themselves, they want to lead and they have the natural urge to instigate action and to initiate.

The fixed signs of Taurus, Leo, Scorpio and Aquarius don't like to be pushed around. If they feel pressurised or challenged they are likely to dig their heels in and not give an inch. Planets in the fixed signs are stable and consistent, and people with predominantly fixed charts tend to be very loyal with a tremendous capacity for endurance and perseverance. There is a strong resistance to change and difficulty letting go, which means that they can get stuck in a rut. On the other hand, planets in the fixed signs can really make things happen, because they have the patience to see things through to their logical conclusion.

The mutable signs of Gemini, Virgo, Sagittarius and Pisces are adaptable, adjustable, changeable and flexible. Planets in these signs tend to be more interested in the journey than in arriving. They also tend to avoid conflict at all costs, because it is not in the nature of the mutable signs to engage in conflict, except as mediators or go-betweens. They will find a way around things and are generally not a bit bothered by changing situations.

Because the modes describe very different orientations, they help us to understand and appreciate why people respond in very different ways to the same situation. I once heard a good example of this. Imagine that three people are travelling along a road – one cardinal, one fixed and one mutable – and that they find the road has been blocked by a huge boulder. Cardinal is likely to see this as an interesting challenge and scale the boulder with climbing equipment, going straight over the top. Mutable simply goes round the outside and carries on, or changes direction altogether and finds another road. Fixed, on the other hand, will spend five years drilling a hole right through the centre.

An image from *Philosophia reformata* (1622) by Johannes Mylius presents us with the four stages or grades of the alchemical work timed according to the Sun's entry into the cardinal signs. The first stage begins in Aries, the second in Cancer and the third in Libra, while the fourth, beginning in Capricorn, symbolises both putrefaction and fermentation

Another example could apply to a classroom situation like ours. Imagine that one evening a completely new tutor arrived who you weren't expecting. Mutable people are likely to think 'OK, this might be interesting, let's go with this and see what happens.' The fixed people are more likely to resist 'We were never told about this, we weren't expecting it and it is not acceptable. I am going to complain.' Cardinal people will probably want to challenge the new tutor to see if they are up to it.

Audience: Would you say that people with the same orientation are likely to be compatible? That the cardinal signs, for example, are likely to get along with each other?

Clare: This is a very interesting question, although the answer is not particularly straightforward. I think it is true to say that with all relationships there is both an attraction of the same and of the different. Unless there is enough similarity we would have no point of contact with the other person. We would be unable to relate to them in any kind of comfortable, familiar way. However, if, as I suspect, relationships are our major vehicle for growth, self-development and self-awareness, then they tend to be most powerful when the partner carries qualities and motivations which are either lacking in our chart or which are in our chart but which we are not expressing for ourselves.

Now if you have a look at the same seven points in your own chart you will discover whether you have any particular modal emphasis. Looking at the example charts, we can see that David has the following modal balance:

Three cardinal: Jupiter and Sun in Aries, Moon in Capricorn
Three fixed: Mars in Leo, Saturn in Aquarius, Mercury in Taurus
One mutable: Venus in Pisces

Sally has the following modal balance:

One cardinal: Mars in Cancer
Four mixed: Saturn in Leo, Mercury, Sun and Venus in Aquarius
Two mutable: Moon in Pisces, Jupiter in Gemini

This distribution immediately gives us clues about David and Sally's natural orientations. David is mostly cardinal and fixed, so he is perfectly capable of setting himself goals (cardinal) and seeing them through to completion (fixed). This is a fairly driven and powerful combination, and there may be times when he needs the input of mutable people, to help him think of alternatives, or ways around and difficulties he has come up against. Sally's natural orientation, on the other hand, is predominantly fixed. She is naturally loyal and reliable and determined (fixed) but is not a natural initiator (lack of cardinal). Does anyone here have a particularly strong cardinal emphasis?

Audience: I have five planets in cardinal signs.

Clare: Do you recognise yourself as someone who has drive? That you are self-determining, self-motivated and goal oriented?

Audience: Well, now that you mention it, I suppose that is right. I do like to be at the wheel, for example. I always have to be the one that drives – literally!

Clare: Exactly. You have just got to lead and be in charge. You are the one who knows where you are going.

Audience: I see myself as a cardinal person, but my chart doesn't agree. I have no planets at all in cardinal signs, but I have always thought of myself as extremely goal oriented. How can that be?

Clare: Well, this is another example of the psyche's inherent compensatory function in the service of our development towards wholeness and personal integration. As we saw when we looked at the principle of polarity, if something is 'missing' from our birth charts, it doesn't mean that it is not there. Rather, it means that it is not an innate part of our conscious awareness of ourselves, so we will meet it in our dealings with the world and with other people, often very powerfully. If you have no cardinal planets in your chart then it is likely that you are not particularly comfortable on a personal level with this particular motivation. In an ideal world, you would prefer that other people make the decisions and lead the way. However, I suspect that as soon as you have dealings with the other world and with other people, circumstances conspire in such a way that you end up feeling compelled to take the lead. With plenty of planets in cardinal signs, this would be instinctive and taken for granted, but with no planets in cardinal signs, it is likely that you feel driven, forced, and compelled and challenged into action. It can become a very compulsive drive or a kind of over-compensation, which can be extremely effective, however uncomfortable. We do tend to find ourselves forced to contend with anything which is missing in our charts.

If you are working with a chart which has a marked lack of a particular polarity or of a particular modality, or even of a particular element, then it is always important to pay attention to this, because it is the imbalances which can provide real clues to the way someone functions in the world. Does anyone have a particular emphasis on the fixed signs?

Audience: Yes, I do.

Clare: So we can assume that you are an extremely reliable person – and that your strengths are being able to stick at something and see it through?

Audience: I am more likely to finish things for other people than for myself. It's a time thing – I only have seven days a week and 24 hours a day, but in the end everything will eventually get done.

Clare: Just listen to that determination. I very much doubt whether a mutable person would have the sticking power to hang around long enough to get everything done. And it is possible that the work you are finishing off for other people was started by cardinal people who have already moved on to their next goal. It is often said that fixed signs finish off what cardinal signs start.

Audience: My sister is a Scorpio and she just won't budge. Ever.

Clare: Isn't it fascinating how different we are? Let's imagine our three people, cardinal, fixed and mutable, planning a holiday. How is each likely to go about it and what kind of holiday would they choose?

Audience: Well I suppose cardinal would like a challenge, like an adventure holiday, but with a goal. Not just sitting on the beach. They might go on a climbing holiday or a cultural tour or a driving rally? At any rate it would probably come naturally to them to do the planning, to get all the information and to make a decision.

Clare: Yes that's right. Mutable is likely to leave it up to others to decide and to organise, and then join in and 'go along for the ride'. Left to their own devices, mutable is unlikely to want to commit to a particular action or destination in advance, and may prefer to leave things open until the last minute and take pot luck, or see if anything else comes up.

If cardinal and mutable are going on holiday together, this could either work very well, with mutable perfectly happy to adapt and adjust to cardinal's plans, or mutable's lack of focus and commitment could just as easily infuriate cardinal. On the other hand, fixed would be resistant to change and may have been to the same place for their holidays for the last 25 years. So I am sure you can see that the issue of where to go on holiday can be a potential minefield.

Audience: I have to argue with you here because virtually all my planets are in fixed signs, and I always want to go somewhere different. I have often been told about this fixed business and how resistant I am to change, but in fact I always need change.

Clare: Just to tease you a little bit, how do you think you would react if your partner suggested that you go back to the same place as last year?

Audience: No, we would need to go somewhere different. OK, I see what you mean – this makes me very fixed and resistant to change!

Clare: Obviously we are just looking at extremes for the time being. These are just caricatures really, and the actual picture is always much more subtle, because it is extremely unusual to find completely pure examples. However, just understanding the difference between these three basic orientations is a tremendous help when it comes to understanding ourselves and others. It helps us to appreciate that everyone has their own particular innate orientation, which may not be the same as ours, but which is equally valid. Each of these three modes has its gifts and qualities and its contribution to make, as well as its more annoying, irritating and difficult aspects. If we can understand someone's orientation, it makes all the difference to our relationship to them.

The Four Elements

Symbolically, the number four finally brings us to the level of manifestation, matter and substance. The word 'nature' means 'that which is born', and all birth into nature is symbolised by the crossing of opposites. This is why we use the term the 'cross of matter', which limits us to our finite physical existence in both time and space, symbolised by the symbol for the Earth itself – the cross within the circle.

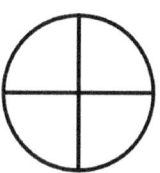

It is the four primary orientations, north, south, east and west, which give us our bearings and which make space and time comprehensible. Every birth chart is also a reflection of the symbol for the Earth, describing precisely the nature of the specific material, solid, concrete world into which each of us is born and through which each of us must manifest ourselves. Our astrological birth charts describe the moment in time and space when each of us takes on a separate physical existence. Whether or not we remain connected to the realms of spirit and soul, from this moment onwards we are literally physically alone in our separate bodies and physically mortal, which implies that one day we will die. The moment of birth is therefore a monumental event, and the moment when our birth charts become 'quartered' by two pairs of opposites – the east/west horizon (ASC/DSC) and the north/south meridian (MC/IC).

It was the Greek philosopher/mathematician Empedocles (c.450 BCE) who first established the system of the four primary elements – fire, air, water and earth. Drawing on the work of his predecessors, his proposal was based very simply and rationally on observation of the qualities of the physical world, which fell into two pairs of opposites: wet and dry, hot and cold. Fire was considered to result from the combination of dry and hot, air was created from the hot and wet, water from the cold and wet, and earth from the cold and dry. Each of the four elements was also associated with one of the four seasons. The earth was seen to be the densest and heaviest element, upon which the water – the sea, lakes and rivers – lay. Both earth and water have mass and weight and their direction is downwards, which explains why these two elements came to be associated with negative, feminine, yin attributes. Above the earth and water is the air with its natural movement upwards, and above the air are the fiery heavens, the Sun, stars and planets, which explains why the elements of air and fire came to be associated with positive, masculine, yang attributes.

The Greeks considered that life itself depends upon a combination of these four elements. Earth is the substance or physical body, and the food which is needed to maintain this existence. Water is essential for life, and the major component of our bodies and of the Earth itself. Respiration, breathing in an out, is another central condition of life, as is the warmth and light of the Sun. Since these four elements existed in the external world, it followed that they also existed within each human being. The life force itself, the force which holds all these four elements together in a discrete living being, is the quintessence, or the fifth principle, or prana, or whatever term we use to describe the life force. It was understood that when a living being died, each of the elements returned to its physical source and the quintessence, or life force, escaped back to its eternal source. This is the basis of the system of the four elements.

Audience: Sorry Clare, but you mentioned five elements, not four?

Clare: The fifth element is known as the 'quintessence', the force itself which holds all of the four elements together in a living being. We could describe the quintessence as including both the spirit and the soul, which are described in the first three levels of the tetractys. At death, the soul is released from the body and is reunited with spirit, with the source from which it originally emerged. These ideas belong to the Hermetic and neo-Platonic schools of thought and have been carried down through the ages by the wisdom traditions. Physical and psychological health was considered to be the result of an elemental balance within the individual, and illness the result of a marked imbalance. The horoscope indicates the natural emphasis of elements we were born with – and any marked imbalance goes a long way towards describing our particular mode of functioning in the world. The idea of the four temperaments, or humours was established around 400 BCE by Hippocrates at the great medical school on the island of Kos. Have a look at this model.

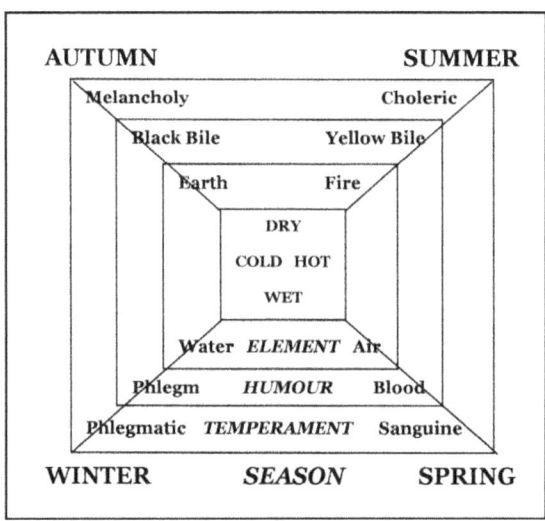

The Elements and the Four Humours

Greek medicine was based on the four humours, a system which was also used to describe the human temperament, psyche and psychology. This system has found its way into our language and, although they are gradually becoming more archaic, we still use the words phlegmatic, sanguine and melancholy to describe someone's 'temperament' or when we refer to someone as being 'temperamental'. Likewise, we still describe a person as being 'in their element' or 'in good humour' or 'out of humour'. You can see from this model how well the psychosomatic connection was originally understood.

Audience: But don't we generally use the term 'psychosomatic' to describe an imaginary illness?

Clare: Yes, that's right, and the term 'psychosomatic' is often used in a derogatory way to describe someone who we believe is a hypochondriac. However, the word literally describes the fundamental connection between the 'psyche' and the 'soma', or the body and the mind, or soul. The Greeks would never have thought of separating the physical from the emotional condition of a patient, and in this sense their medicine was truly holistic. This system of classification was used throughout medieval and renaissance Europe and sits very comfortably alongside astrology. Indeed, it was a requirement for physicians to study astrology as part of their training.

Audience: They still do that in some places.

The Four Elements in Astrology

Now that we have reached the level of the four elements we can add the final layer to the descriptions of the twelve zodiac signs. Once again, the descriptions of our elemental and psychological typology are reflected in our language. The element of earth is literally tangible, solid, stable, dependable, reliable, supportive, heavy and concrete. And these are the same words we might use to describe a person with an emphasis of planets in earth signs. We might even say that they are 'well grounded' or have their 'feet on the ground' or are 'down to earth'. Equally, in birth charts where the earth element is weak or absent, we might be tempted to suggest that they 'get real' or that they are 'unearthed'. Fire is literally hot, devouring, radiant, volatile, expansive and explosive. All these words can be used to describe a person with an emphasis of planets in fire signs. Air can be breezy, draughty, dry or stale, words which can be used to describe a person with an emphasis of planets in air signs. Such a person might be 'a breath of fresh air' or 'full of hot air' (a combination of fire and air) or have a 'dry sense of humour'. Water is wet, fluid, flowing, dissolving, flooding, dripping, stormy, supportive and healing, all words which describe a person with an emphasis of planets in water signs. Such a person might be described as a 'drip' or 'wet' or 'fluid'.

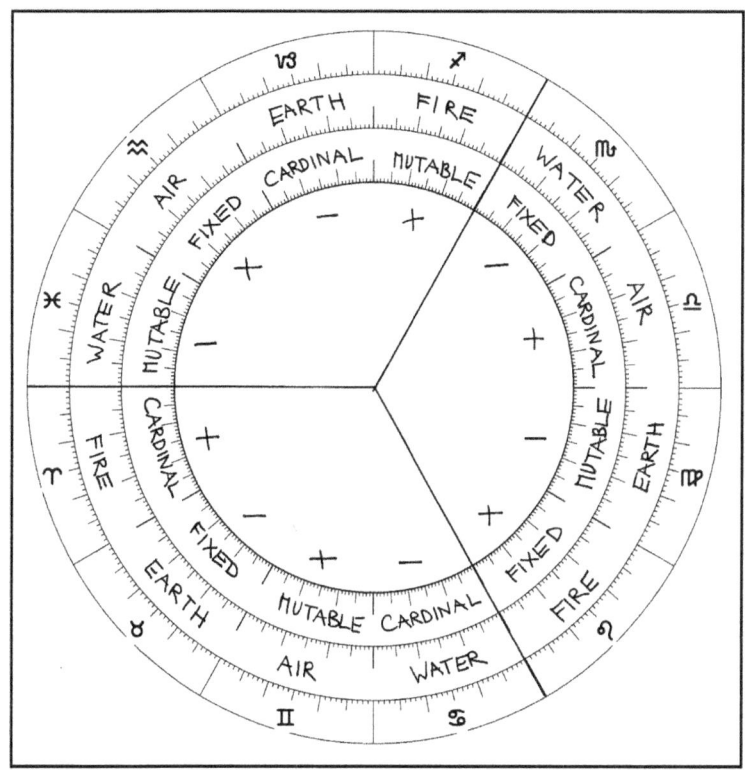

FIRE
Enthusiastic, confident, dramatic
Aries ♈, Leo ♌, Sagittarius ♐

EARTH
Practical, realistic, reliable
Taurus ♉, Virgo ♍, Capricorn ♑

AIR
Detached, objective, rational, abstract
Gemini ♊, Libra ♎, Aquarius ♒

WATER
Sensitive, emotional, receptive
Cancer ♋, Scorpio ♏, Pisces ♓

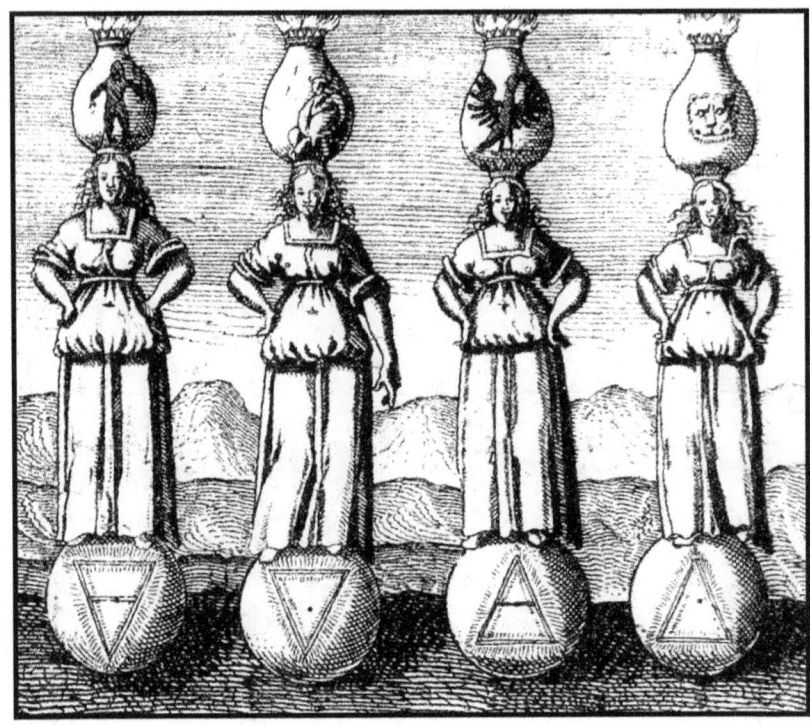

The four elements in alchemy are portrayed in Johann Daniel Mylius' *Philosophia reformata* (1622) as representing the four stages of the alchemical *opus*. From left to right are earth, water, air and fire.

Jung's Psychological Types

For Jung, the number four, or the quaternity, provided a description of the way the conscious mind takes its bearings:

> Four as the minimal number by which order can be created represents the pluralistic state of the man who has not yet attained inner unity, hence the state of bondage and disunion, of disintegration, and of being torn in different directions – an agonizing, unredeemed state which longs for union, reconciliation, redemption, healing and wholeness.[2]

Jung's model of the four psychological types is expressed as two pairs of opposites:

Modes and Elements 139

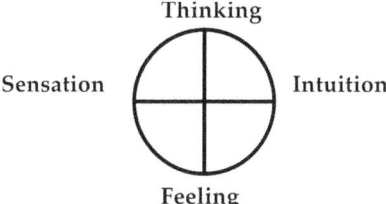

As you can see from this diagram of the fourfold structure of the psyche, the Intuition function is the polar opposite of the Sensation function and the Thinking function is the polar opposite of the Feeling function. Although there are undoubtedly strong parallels between different fourfold models of the psyche, it is important not to try and reduce them to each other, since each has its own internal integrity. For Jung 'It is one's psychological type which from the outset determines and limits a person's judgment.'[3] Psychological types are classes or groups of people with similar reaction patterns, typical attitudes that constitute:

> .... an essential bias which conditions the whole psychic process, establishes the habitual reactions, and thus determines not only the style of behaviour, but also the nature of subjective experience. And not only so, but it also denotes the kind of compensatory activity of the unconscious which we may expect to find.[4]

Jung believed that if a particular psychological function was conscious and well developed, it was likely that the opposite function would remain unconscious, unknown and undifferentiated, containing powerful 'shadow' qualities which can often end up dominating the life of that individual. Intuitives are therefore likely to have a Sensation shadow and vice versa, and Thinking types are likely to have a Feeling shadow and vice versa.

There is an analogy between this system and the psychological expression of the four elements in astrology. Strongly developed fire types will often have an earth shadow and vice versa and strongly developed air types will often have a water shadow and vice versa. We will look at this more closely when we come to study the particular elements themselves. Of course, if we are lucky enough to have two opposite functions well-developed and conscious then they can function very, very effectively together. However, as is normally the case with opposites, one side of the spectrum tends to be either projected, or unconscious, in which case it will often fall into the shadow.

Audience: You are using the term shadow to describe something which is unconscious?

Clare: Yes, because it is repressed. Given that the psyche is, in principle at least, capable of being in balance and harmony, anything which remains unconscious does not simply go away, but falls into the shadow, from where it takes on a life of its own, unmediated by the ego. Our shadow qualities are often extremely obvious to others but, unfortunately, never to ourselves. Alternatively, we will 'project' our shadows onto the world or onto other people, not seeing these qualities as parts of our own psyche, since anything which we don't recognise in ourselves we tend to meet in the outside world.

Audience: So our task is to make all the elements conscious, whether or not we have planets in each of the elements?

Clare: Yes, that is true, assuming we are all striving to become fully conscious, whole and complete, although whether this is actually possible is another matter! Certainly we can become much more self aware by knowing our own personal psychological biases, and less likely to blame the world or other people for our own failings, but this is very difficult indeed to do.

Audience: So we cut off our shadows, and then find that we are confronted with them anyway?

Clare: Exactly. Now, at the risk of overwhelming you with too many fourfold models all at once, there is one more I want to introduce before we move on to discuss the signs of the zodiac. It provides a further dimension, a description of four different types of truth, which I think is very valid to astrology. This is found in the quadrant model devised by the contemporary writer and integrative psychologist/philosopher Ken Wilber.

For Wilber,[5] the quest for knowledge 'has almost universally consisted of two different and apparently conflicting paths', our *subjective experience* of the world and our *objective descriptions* of the world, which appear to be at odds with each other:

	Subjective	**Objective**
Individual	[Fire]	[Earth]
Collective	[Water]	[Air]

The Four Faces of Truth

For Wilber there are two different types of subjective experience, individual and collective. Individual, subjective experience refers to personal meaning, interpretation, values and truth. Collective, subjective experience refers to our shared sense of belonging, shared values and mutual understandings. The right hand side of this model describes two different approaches to objective reality, one individual and one collective. Individual objective reality arrives at the truth via 'empirical deduction from objectively observable facts'. Collective objective reality concerns whole systems such as large organisations, field theory, etc.

The quadrant model above appears to provide a remarkably accurate description of the relative 'truths' of each of the four elements, which I have added to the diagram above. Wilber writes that each of these quadrants has its own truth and its own language, which form a crucial part of the whole picture. Each has its particular contribution to make and its particular weaknesses. The aim of the integrative approach is to become aware of each of these domains. 'If any system of thought attempts to ignore or deny any of the four validity claims, then those ignored truths actually reappear in the system as an internal and massive self contradiction.'[6] If we can understand that each of these orientations is equally valid and that none of them possesses the whole truth, then we are much more likely to be able to understand both ourselves and others, and less likely to judge or blame others for not being like us.

Now that we have set the scene by exploring the general meaning of the polarities, modes and elements separately, we are ready to move on to explore the zodiac signs themselves.

Notes

1. See Edward C. Whitmont, *The Symbolic Quest*, p.228.
2. C. G. Jung, *The Psychology of the Transference*, p.46.
3. C. G. Jung, *Memories, Dreams and Reflections*, p.207.
4. C. G. Jung, *Psychological Types*, p.547.
5. Ken Wilber, *The Eye of Spirit: An Integral Vision for a World Gone Slightly Mad*.
6. Ibid.

LESSON 9

The Fire and Earth Signs

I want to look at the fire and earth signs together because, as opposite elements, they both challenge and complement each other. It makes it easier to grasp the meaning of an element if we compare it to what it is not. Fire is positive and masculine, earth is negative and feminine. Using Wilber's quadrant model, these two elements share the same personal, individual orientation to the world. For fire, this orientation is personal and subjective. An example of this would be a religious experience or personal conviction, which is absolutely real to the individual but which cannot be, and does not need to be proved, explained or justified, since it is true for the individual. For the earth signs, the truth is objective, but just as personal, arising from earth's own experience, via the five senses, of the outside world. For example, if earth doesn't like the smell, taste or colour of something, then that is that. Nobody can argue otherwise. If we can really understand how each element experiences and interprets the world, then we can appreciate that each element has its place as part of a greater whole.

Fire is, of course, hot, but it is also magnetic – it pulls us in. If you have ever stood watching a bonfire or sat around an open fire, I am sure you will have experienced this fascination. As we watch the flames, they pull us into a trancelike state which leads us away from the 'real world' and into our imaginations. It is in our imaginations that the visions, myths and fantasies of fire are most at home. Our imaginations lead us into a world where everything is exaggerated, colourful, larger than life and full of exciting potential. It is from the imagination that fire signs draw their contagious warmth and enthusiasm, fired by a unique and personal connection to a grand vision, a quest, a big picture which sets the stage for their own lives.

The fire signs have an enthusiastic, spontaneous child-like quality. Fire is exaggerated, larger than life, and fire signs need to – and must, if they are to be true to themselves – live right at the centre of their own individual dramas and mythic dreams. Fire signs have an innate sense of their own unique specialness, which explains why they have a tremendous faith in themselves and why they will take the kind of risks that other elements shrink from, since they believe intrinsically that they will be lucky, or 'specially favoured' in some way. 'Objective truths', such as the statistical odds against winning the lottery, for example, are meaningless to fire signs and often a cause of incomprehension, frustration and impatience. Even when things don't turn out as planned, even when they crash and burn, fire signs normally have the faith to pick themselves up and carry on. For the element of fire, relationships are about the excitement and fascination of the chase, the as yet unconsummated desire for an object – be it another person or an ideal. Fire cannot and will not be contained or restricted – it is not concerned with commitment and stability. This explains why so many people get burned when they 'play with fire'.

In alchemical imagery the element of fire is represented by the salamander, which was believed to endure the heat of the flames because of the coolness of its body. This salamander is from Michael Maier's *Atalanta fugiens* (1618).

The other interesting thing about the elements is that, in a very concrete way, we use up our main element quickly and need to replenish it constantly in order to keep our energy levels up. This is why, on a very basic level, people with an emphasis on fire in their charts really need plenty of sunshine, since the Sun, which is the physical manifestation of fire in our solar system, actually restores their energy levels and their vitality. Fire signs also need to replenish and restore themselves through physical exercise, travel and adventure, or by going to the theatre, a rock concert or to the opera – since they need plenty of drama and fantasy. These experiences will not only restore their energy levels, but also their basic optimism in life. When fire gets what it needs, its warm spontaneity and instinctive generosity is enormously healing for others, although fire signs themselves are often unaware of this fact, since it is simply a by-product of their natural vitality. On the other hand, if you don't have much fire then you might find that fire people drain your energy because they are simply 'too much' to be around. Your job will be to learn how to play, how to have fun, which is not an easy thing to do if it doesn't come naturally.

Audience: This is all very well, but it is not the real world, is it?

Clare: Well, that depends where you are coming from. For fire this is in fact the real world, but your comment is a good illustration of the fact that each element evokes its opposite. Is there anyone else who is feeling that all this enthusiasm and faith needs to be contained or disciplined?

Audience: It sounds to me as if the fire signs are rather selfish and insensitive.

Clare: Well, from the point of view of the earth element you are right. If we keep strictly to the basic meaning of fire and earth, what does earth do to fire?

Audience: Puts it out. Smothers it, suffocates it.

Clare: Exactly. And yet the paradox is that fire cannot burn unless it is consuming some kind of matter, such as coal or wood, both of which belong to the earth element. This explains both the repulsion and attraction that exists between fire and earth. They are opposites but they need each other. We can understand why earth resists and seeks to control fire, which threatens to consume it – burn it up. On the other hand, earth needs fire, which is the life force itself. I believe that there is a species of eucalyptus tree in Australia which needs intense heat – a forest fire – before it can burst forth into life and new growth again. Another example is of the mythic bird, the phoenix, which, in order to be reborn, needs to enter into the fire on a regular basis and be totally consumed, or purified, by the fire.

By contrast, the earth signs are rooted in here and now tangible reality. They are solid, dependable, practical and reliable, concerned with the material world and with the five senses. Think of earth literally; everything that supports us grows from the earth, all the food we eat comes from the earth. Earth supports life and the earth signs have very strong security needs and tend to be very conservative. They are realistic. They are able to manifest, to make things happen, and have a tremendous ability for perseverance and endurance. The earth signs come into their own when realism and practical solutions are called for.

The earth signs tend to be comfortable and in touch with the natural world and, unlike the other elements, tend not to repress or undervalue the body's needs for proper nourishment, rest and exercise. Of all the elements, the earth signs are the most sensual and sexual. Earth is in its element here. Many fire signs, on the other hand, have an active dislike of their bodies, which are too confining, too restrictive. Our bodies hold us back, and they need to be fed, clothed and rested.

Audience: So what are the limitations of earth?

Clare: In general terms, the limitations of the earth signs are the same as the strengths of the fire signs. The practical, realistic earth signs can have a marked lack of enthusiasm, hope, faith and optimism, which can result in a kind of cynical disappointment with life, a sense that the world has 'let them down'. There can also be a lack of imagination and the inability to think symbolically. Taken to extremes, the 'concrete thinker' can become evangelical or fundamentalist, which tends to be an expression not of faith, but of its lack.

The Fire and Earth Signs 147

The element of earth is shown in Johann Daniel Mylius' *Philosophia reformata* (1622) as the primal substance, suckling the baby *filius philosophorum*, the alchemical gold. On the left is the salamander of the element of fire, and to the right the birds of the element of air.
Earth stands with her feet in the element of water

Equally, the limitations of the fire signs can be described as the strengths of the earth signs. The difficulties, for fire signs, are the thousand obstacles of a practical nature which threaten to spoil and obstruct the fantasy. They can have problems coping with ordinary, everyday matters. The world has a tendency to frustrate fire, with all its boring details, red tape, traffic laws, bills, regulations and other demands, not to mention other people who point out, practically but not very helpfully, all the very good reasons why something is not possible. Fiery people can feel panicked and really miserable by a tax return and will do anything to escape. In a curious way, a tax return is an affront to fire, which doesn't see the need to justify its existence to anyone or to obey the rules which, after all, only apply to ordinary mortals! Fire signs are not interested in the actual reality of the situation, which is why they cannot necessarily remember where they put their car keys or tend to leave the house without any money.

The fiery imagination can travel anywhere, without limitation. Fire can imagine being in the Andes climbing mountains, or swimming with dolphins off the coast of New Zealand, or travelling in a spaceship to the outer reaches of the solar system, or on a ten year retreat in a Japanese Zen monastery, but in order to turn these dreams into reality the practical element of earth is needed. We have to earn enough money in order to be able to afford to turn our dreams into reality, and we have to navigate train and plane timetables, remember to get our visas updated and leave enough time to get to the airport if we are not to miss our plane.

Earth is not the only challenge to fire. The air and water signs can be equally obstructive. Fire's subjective vision and enthusiasm can easily be crushed by air's rational analysis of the actual facts, and water can douse the heat and enthusiasm. Fire signs can be very vulnerable and tend to have a curious lack of stamina. They can easily be overwhelmed by the resistances which the world throws at them, and it is not unusual to meet fire signs who seem to have been 'put out'.

Audience: Isn't that because they are rather selfish and out of control?

Clare: That is exactly the reaction or the judgement which they tend to invoke. There is a tendency to try and restrict all this enthusiasm by putting boundaries around it, and if this happens early in life or too insensitively, then it can have a lasting effect on the life force of the individual or can break their will to the extent that they cease to believe in themselves. In this case, the astrologer has work to do. Unless the natural enthusiasm, optimism and self belief of the fire element can be rekindled, it may become distorted; violent and destructive, in the case of Aries, demanding and jealous in the case of Leo, or arrogant and patronising in the case of Sagittarius.

Audience: So if this happens then presumably the fire signs need a new vision and a new quest or adventure?

Clare: Yes, at the end of the day they must believe in themselves and need others to believe in them.

ARIES
Cardinal Fire
Ruler: Mars
Exaltation: Sun
Detriment: Venus
Fall: Saturn

Each of the elements becomes progressively more 'mature' in the order of the zodiac signs. For example, the first fire sign of Aries is cardinal, a very primal force. The second fire sign is fixed – Leo is a calmer, steadier expression of fire. The third fire sign is mutable, Sagittarius, reaching outwards and beyond to find meaning through exploration of the wider spectrum, the broader picture.

Aries is the infant of the zodiac – the sign of the spring equinox and of all new beginnings. It is an extremely straightforward and uncomplicated sign, pure naïve energy and courage. Ruled by Mars, Aries is forceful, instinctive and immediate – when he wants something, he wants it now. Aries rules the head and leads with the head, often literally walking head first, leaning forwards for speed and focus. Aries can be associated with head-butting, but also with leading intellectually. In common with all the fire signs, Aries can appear to trample on other people's feelings and sensitivities without even noticing, but there is nothing devious or malicious about the sign. It is too primal and spontaneous for that. If they have hurt someone they will be surprised, it is just that they don't instinctively consider other people's feelings. There is not a great deal of subtlety with Aries, they are very black and white, either/or.

Planets in Aries do not suffer from doubt because, as the pure primal subjective energy of the first sign of the zodiac, nothing else and nobody else exists outside his vision, his goal and his quest. Naturally, there are many people who find all this single-minded focus and determination rather brutal and selfish. But, like all fire signs, Aries is gripped by a heroic vision. He needs a challenge or a battlefield in which there is everything to play for, and no time to wait.

Audience: I don't know if you have seen the film *Troy*, but there is a moment when Achilles decides to fight on the Greek side against Troy and he and his men join the thousand ships sailing towards Troy, but he does it on his own terms and must be the first to reach the shore and to engage in battle.

Clare: Yes, this is an excellent example of pure Aries energy – foolhardy, heroic and goal oriented. And of course Achilles was chasing immortality – he didn't care whether or not he was killed. Nor did he care whether the Greeks or the Trojans won the war at the end of the day. This was irrelevant to his own personal quest. What was important is that he achieved his immortality, established a mythic identity for himself. And here we are thousands of years later talking about him, so it must have worked.

The Greek myths are full of good examples of heroic Aries figures. For example Jason, who led the Argonauts on the quest for the golden fleece; Theseus, who led his men to Crete and overcame the Minotaur; Perseus, whose quest involved the rescue of Andromeda, chained to the rocks as a sacrifice to Poseidon. All these heroes are instinctive leaders, goal-oriented, daring and brave. No matter how foolhardy, there is always something noble about the venture, the quest and the vision. There are codes of honour and chivalry attached, which, in the case of Aries, often involve the rescuing of a damsel in distress along the way.

Audience: What about Robin Hood? He sounds like an Aries character.

Clare: Exactly. All the components are there. He was a natural and instinctive leader of his band of outlaws, and he had a noble vision to steal from the rich and give to the poor. This was his quest – very simple and effective. And of course the maiden in distress in this case was Maid Marion. Joan of Arc is a female example of the Aries personality. God spoke to her, which is perfectly possible if you are a fire sign. From the moment she was given her quest she was ablaze with determination to lead the French to victory against the English and to rescue the French dauphin.

Audience: And eventually she was burned at the stake.

Clare: Exactly, and she also became immortal to the extent that she is still a symbol of the female warrior hundreds of years later.

Planets in Aries
David has both the Sun and Jupiter in Aries. Let's have a look at that. As I mentioned before, the Sun is always one of the hardest planets to interpret, since it has so many levels of interpretation and is, ultimately, the experience of personal integrity and authenticity as well as our connection to our spiritual identity and purpose. On a personal level, the Sun in Aries will describe David's impression of his father, who normally carries the archetypal projection of the Sun in our youth, before we are mature enough to integrate it for ourselves. David will identify with all the qualities of Aries which we have already noted. He will be competitive, goal oriented and impatient, and will need to choose and follow his own path. He will have that quality of honour and nobility, which is a feature of all the fire signs.

Ultimately, since the Sun describes the mature centre of David's being and of his identity, I have found that a useful psychological approach is to focus on the conscious integration of the qualities of the Sun's opposite sign and on the development of the planets which are traditionally in their detriment and fall in the Sun's sign. A more measured, mature expression of the Aries Sun will be the balancing of his own will and instinctive, hot headed subjectivity with a genuine consideration for, and sensitivity to, the needs of others, so that he comes to fight not just for himself but for the broader values of justice, peace and harmony (Libra). This will bring Venus (ruler of Libra) into a creative relationship with Mars (ruler of Aries) and the maturity and nobility of the Sun will provide Aries with the wisdom, integrity and authority to be a good and noble leader.

As far as Jupiter in Aries is concerned, a useful shorthand technique is to think of the planet as the 'what', and the sign it falls in as the 'how'. So, in this case we know that Jupiter is the principle of expansion, faith and optimism, it tells us what is meaningful for a particular individual. Jupiter in Aries tells us that David will believe in self-reliance, self-motivation and goal-orientation, the more challenging the goal the better, and that he will achieve a sense of personal meaning, fulfilment and purpose when he engages in any kind of self-imposed challenge.

Audience: I have Jupiter in Aries and I definitely go along my own path.

Clare: So we could certainly say that you believe (Jupiter) in doing your own thing (Aries).

Audience: My brother has the Moon in Aries and he was the problem child in the family – always in trouble.

Clare: The Moon is what feeds us and makes us feel safe, so if we want to know how he gets what he needs, we can see that he will do this by competing and challenging and fighting in order to assert his will and his need for autonomy. Literally, we could say that your brother needs (Moon) to fight (Aries). Naturally, if he is born into a gentle, peace loving family, he will become the problem child. If, on the other hand, he was born into a highly competitive family, this quality may well be admired and encouraged. It all depends on the context.

Moon in Aries describes spontaneous emotional responses, quick reactions, a short fuse and a hot temper. It is instinctively competitive and needs immediate gratification. Moon in Aries also eats quickly, as if every meal is a challenge or a race. Meal times can be the arena for family fights. I have often noticed that people with Moon in Aries burn off their food quickly and get to the point where they are suddenly completely empty, drained and must eat NOW. In common with all the fire signs, generally there can be a surprising lack of stamina. Does that sound like your brother?

Audience: Absolutely! He always finishes his food before anyone else, and family mealtimes with him around are a nightmare – a real battleground.

Audience: I have Venus in Aries, but I have always assumed it doesn't work well there because it is in its detriment.

Clare: This is an important point, which illustrates how I think a psychological approach differs from a more traditional approach. Venus describes an individual's values, talents and joys. Placed in Aries, a psychological interpretation would be that you find joy through expressing your natural instinctive urge for leadership, competition and the achievement of personal goals. This placement indicates a love (Venus) of the fight (Aries), a valuing (Venus) of strength and determination and courage (Aries) so, from this point of view, Venus is just as happy in Aries as in any other sign. The sign simply describes how the planet will find its best expression. Venus in Aries enjoys the chase and loves to fight for something. She is competitive in relationships and values the qualities of courage, determination and leadership in herself and in others. Venus in Aries is also likely to value her freedom and autonomy. We could even say that this is a powerful Venus because she knows what she wants.

LEO
Fixed Fire
Ruler: The Sun
Detriment: Saturn

Leo is fixed fire – an interesting paradox. Perhaps the best way to describe fixed fire is in terms of its ruler – the Sun, the constant and predictable source of light and life at the centre of the solar system, around which all the planets revolve. Leo is associated with the metal gold and with incorruptible, eternal fire. This is exactly how planets in Leo function best – when they are radiating their unique life force for the benefit of all. Leo has a great warmth, an ability to shine and an immense generosity. There is something very sunny about Leo. There is also a natural dignity and nobility, an extravagance, a love of luxury and of doing things in style. Leo rules the back and the heart, and the back is to do with being vertical isn't it. You can often recognise a Leo from the dignified way they carry themselves, as if they had a crown on their heads. Sometimes there is something very catlike and delicate about the way they walk.

Leos are proud, we talk about a pride of lions, don't we? They prefer to be leaned on than to lean on or depend on others. They are very good at giving magnanimous advice but not so good at taking it. Leo is an extremely good delegator and likes to be surrounded by courtiers who will carry out his requests. This is a perfectly natural expectation for Leo, who instinctively expects to be waited on, served and cleaned up after.

And this quality, which is present to some extent in all the fire signs, can annoy other people intensely: 'Who does he think he is?'

Audience: But they don't like to be pushed around, do they?

Clare: That's right, because we are talking about a fixed sign here. Leo will resist being forced to do anything he doesn't want to do, he will resist change. Remember that fire signs are subjective and imaginative, and Leo exists in the centre of his own myth, as the special one, the unique one, as the 'divine child' of the zodiac. The most important world to Leo is the drama in which he plays the leading role. In this sense, Leos are not ordinary mortals. In their imaginations they are always on stage in the limelight in front of hundreds of admiring, adoring people. Recognition and praise is their birthright.

The more insecure Leo who does not really believe in himself, will be unable to shine or radiate from his own heart and may become desperate for the approval of others and demand recognition and praise as a substitute for a lack of genuine self worth. The worst thing that can happen to a Leo is humiliation, which is an absolutely devastating experience. If Leo is repeatedly humiliated during childhood, then they can shut their hearts to avoid feeling any repeated pain. They are vulnerable to being crushed, to having their innate sense of specialness destroyed.

Audience: Sorry Clare, where did you say this crushing comes from?

Clare: Perhaps it is the natural result of each element evoking its opposite element. Fire evokes an earth reaction, which tends to kill the fantasy by being practical and realistic, by throwing up hurdles and resistances and taking the wind out of fire's sails. The world will tend to withhold recognition until Leo has proved itself. This is perfectly reasonable. For example, it is unlikely that a boy will actually grow up to play rugby or football for England unless he puts in the training. Or that we will be appointed to the post of university professor without having done the necessary degrees. In the end, we all have to work for our achievements if they are to hold any value to us. Ultimately, it is the practical harnessing of the element of earth which supports and hones and shapes the true potential of the fire signs.

Planets in Leo

The Sun-in-Leo's lifetime journey is to grow towards the mature realisation and expression of personal authenticity, integrity and authority which is not dependent on the opinions of others. The integration of the planet Saturn, in its detriment in Leo, is an important clue that, over time and through real concrete achievements, the spontaneous childlike quality of Leo will mature until Leo Sun becomes the strong and radiant centre of its own existence. The integration of the opposite sign of Aquarius indicates that, ultimately, Leos have an important part to play which is for the benefit of the larger community. The Disney film *The Lion King* is an excellent example of the difficult and challenging journey towards the mature expression of the Leo Sun, and I would certainly recommend that you see this film. If a Leo Sun ceases to believe in themselves, or tries to take the easy way, then everything starts to go wrong.

Our case study David has Mars in Leo. How do you think this will manifest? Remember that Mars describes the 'what' and Leo will tell us 'how'.

Audience: Well, Mars is about action, potency and outward directed energy. Perhaps David will devote a great deal of energy into getting recognition and admiration?

Clare: Absolutely. There is something very bold and dramatic about this placement. He may even be the driving force behind setting up an amateur dramatics group, in which he will of course cast himself in the leading role. Sally, on the other hand, has Saturn in Leo. If Saturn describes what we crave but feel we have been denied, it also describes the lessons we need to learn in order to gain a sense of genuine self confidence and mastery over our lives. It is possible that Sally has never been made to feel special, or received the kind of attention or praise that she craves. Her self confidence may be low and she will have a fear of being humiliated, which will make her cautious about putting herself forward. Ultimately she can learn to take responsibility for herself and gain self confidence through her concrete achievements. The mantra: 'If I am not for myself, who is?' can encourage Saturn in Leo to believe that they have as much right as anyone else to a place in the Sun.

The lion in alchemy is the primitive, untransmuted form of the alchemical gold. The processes of the *opus* transform it into the reborn *filius philosophorum*, the goal of the work. This image from Lambsprinck's *De lapide philosophica* (1625) portrays the lion and lioness as the male and female sides of the primal substance.

Audience: I have Uranus in Leo.

Clare: Uranus was in Leo for the seven years from 1955 to 1962. How many of you have this? Quite a few. This is an interesting placement because Uranus is egalitarian and Leo is about being special and unique, so there is an inherent conflict here.

Using a shorthand approach, we can say that Uranus describes what a particular group of people don't believe in, what they rebel against, will want to challenge and break down in order to establish a new, more ideal order. In Leo we could say that Uranus is the urge to be republican, they want to break up old elitisms, like the monarchy, and challenge any system based on undeserved privilege, such as the House of Lords. At the same time this generation will have unusual and radical and shocking ways of expressing themselves, and the punk generation is a good example of this group, Mohicans, safety pins and all. On an individual level, it is possible that the ideology of this group could undermine their belief in their own personal recognition. For example, in the workplace Uranus in Leo may hold themselves back if it is against their principles to be promoted over others. On the other hand, being in a position of responsibility could give them the power to establish new, more egalitarian, team-based working practices. So there is always a kind of double bind when the outer planets are concerned, and it is important for the individual to make personal choices rather than simply becoming an unconscious mouthpiece of the collective ideology into which they were born.

SAGITTARIUS
Mutable Fire
Ruler: Jupiter
Detriment: Mercury

The mutable fire sign of Sagittarius is the most mature, but also the most restless and expansive of the fire signs. With Jupiter as its ruling planet, Sagittarius is always seeking the bigger picture, the meaning of life, greater wisdom, more knowledge, more adventures into the unknown and more experiences. It is the journey itself, rather than the goal, which is important for this mutable sign. Sagittarius refuses to be trapped either physically or intellectually and as soon as, or even before, something threatens to become mundane or routine, they will be off to the next thing, chasing the next horizon which holds fascinating future possibilities for something even more meaningful. As king of the gods, Jupiter was larger than life, flamboyant, spontaneous, reactive, with an explosive temper, hurling thunderbolts when he was angry. The sheer scale of Sagittarius, its generosity and benevolence, its gales, hurricanes and tornadoes, can be overwhelming, and the explosive temper, quickly spent, can nevertheless leave the more sensitive signs shaken for some time afterwards.

This sign often has a tremendous amount of physical energy and a strong constitution, and physical exercise and sport can be a positive way to work off this energy. Sagittarians have no natural boundaries, which explains why they are often so clumsy, crashing into things and into other people. Fundamentally sociable and gregarious, Sagittarians tend to sweep up other people into their orbit. The more people, the bigger the party, the better. They will always be seeking a more universal or philosophical dimension to life. Their vision is so powerful that, with the self confidence of all the fire signs, they can even come to believe that they are the arbiters of the one and only truth, which opens them up to accusations of being arrogant, patronising and condescending.

The integration of the opposite sign of Gemini and of the planet Mercury, in its detriment in this sign, can bring a more objective, rational approach and an appreciation of the possibility that truths can be partial and multiple and that other, equally valid opinions and views exist. The integration of Mercury can bring a sense of humour and detachment to what can otherwise become a rather overwhelming, evangelical approach to life.

Planets in Sagittarius
Audience: I have Venus in Sagittarius and I certainly love to travel.

Clare: Absolutely. If you put Venus in Sagittarius in an office, she will go crazy.

Audience: Yes, actually that's true, I do go crazy in offices.

Clare: A frustrated Venus is always dangerous, because if she doesn't get what she wants she becomes extremely disruptive. One of the ways you might escape from an office situation is to start arguments and spread chaos until you are fired, in other words, until you get your freedom.

Audience: That's true. Really true. I didn't realise that's what I was doing.

Audience: I have Mercury in Sagittarius, and I suppose that means I talk a lot?

Clare: Yes, and also you may find yourself embellishing or exaggerating what you say, turning otherwise ordinary events into a drama, into theatre, feeding the fire. So for example, the weather will be absolutely terrible, an ordinary unfortunate event will be a complete disaster, a holiday will have been fantastic, amazing, wonderful – all big words. Mercury in Sagittarius is also said to have 'foot in mouth' disease, the tendency to speak before thinking, and to interrupt. On the other hand it is highly intuitive. There is an extraordinary ability to perceive and anticipate the future, what lies around the next corner.

Let's have a look at the Neptune in Sagittarius in Sally's chart, since many of you are likely to share this placement. Neptune was in Sagittarius for 14 years from November 1970 to January 1984, and again briefly between June and November 1984. Neptune describes our collective dreams and longings for a more ideal world, what we are thirsty for, what we look to for spiritual redemption and salvation and what illusions and fantasies we are particularly susceptible to. For the Neptune in Sagittarius generation the longed for ideas lie somewhere 'out there', beyond the scope of our ordinary lives. There can be an idealisation of foreign lands and countries, travel and exploration and people from different religions and cultures than our own.

From a personal point of view this placement can be very painful, since it can indicate a dissatisfaction and refusal to accept what is actually possible, an inability to settle for one's lot which can condemn the individual to a life where any kind of commitment can be seen as second best, because whatever one is seeking for belongs somewhere else, if only they could find it. On the other hand, if there is a sufficiently well developed ego structure, which can withstand the force of Neptune's tendency to drown us, then we could say that this generation has a genuine connection to a way of being which is more meaningful and inclusive, and that they can be the carriers of these ideals for the benefit of the collective.

The time has come for us to leave the mythic world of fire and to come down to earth. I think it is important to realise that, collectively, we are losing our natural connection to the earth and our sense of belonging to and being a part of nature. Collectively, the qualities of fire are admired and encouraged, whereas the qualities of earth are misunderstood and undervalued. For the last 200 years at least, we have been plundering the earth's resources and increasingly developing the power to control and manipulate nature. We are also doing this to our bodies, which are often seen as the 'enemy' ready to strike back with illness and disease unless they are fiercely controlled and disciplined. Our natural connection to the earth and to living nature has been overtaken and distorted by the widespread materialism, consumerism and need for ownership which is such a feature of modern life. All this tells us that the earth function needs to be collectively redeemed. The earth signs can help us preserve our connection with the natural world and from this point of view we have much to learn from them.

TAURUS
Fixed Earth
Ruler: Venus
Exaltation: Moon
Detriment: Mars

Earth is a negative feminine element and as the earth signs unfold from Taurus to Virgo to Capricorn, they describe successively more mature expressions of this element. Taurus is fixed earth, which tells us that it is the most solid of all the signs. Ruled by Venus, with the Moon in its exaltation, these two feminine planets give Taurus its charming, gentle nature. Venus rules two of the signs of the zodiac – the feminine, 'being', fixed earth sign of Taurus and the masculine, 'doing', cardinal air sign of Libra. This fact tells us that there are two fundamentally different ways in which Venus finds expression, as both an active and a passive principle. An excellent example of the principle of Venus as the ruler of Taurus is the Botticelli painting of Aphrodite, goddess of love and beauty, in *The Birth of Venus*, which I am sure is known to you all.

Audience: She is very beautiful.

Clare: Yes, she is an expression of the Renaissance ideal of earthly beauty, standing naked on a shell, with the winds blowing her gently onto the shore.

Audience: Wasn't she born from the severed testicles of Uranus?

Clare: That's right, she was born out of terrible bloodshed and conflict. Here you can see the central importance of the relationship between strife and love, or Mars and Venus. Without the preceding violence and destruction, Venus would not have been born in the first place. In order for anything to be in balance and harmony there needs to be a relationship between these two principles. The point about this Venus principle is that it is sensual, fertile and passionate. There is an ability to delight in the good things of life and a real capacity for enjoyment. As the principle of love, beauty and pleasure, the Taurean Venus encourages us to validate and fulfil our personal values and desires. This is not particularly easy to do in our puritan culture, but as a symbol of self worth, knowing what gives us pleasure and joy, Venus gives us the power to draw towards us what we desire.

As a fixed earth sign, Taurus is strongly connected to the natural world and to the rhythms of the growth cycles and the seasons. There is a real need for contact with nature, which is why Taureans are often farmers or gardeners, florists or artists working with natural materials, such as sculptors, or using their bodies as their instruments, in the case of singers and dancers. One of the male images of Taurus is that of the green man, the male fertility principle. The feast of Beltane, which takes place in Taurus time, at the beginning of May, is an ancient celebration of fertility held when the crops are beginning to establish themselves and the vegetation is becoming lush and green. Taurus is a very sensuous sign, relating to themselves and to the world through the five senses of sight, touch, smell, hearing and taste. Taureans normally love the feel of silk, satin, fur and velvet, feel happy when they are surrounded by nature and beautiful colours, fine wines, good food, pleasant smells, such as perfume or coffee or the scent of flowers, and music The relationship to the senses and to the physical body is a source of real joy and delight for Taureans. There is normally a kind of serenity and calmness about this gentle, peace-loving sign, and often a real grace and beauty about the way they move. The actress Audrey Hepburn and the ballerina Darcy Bussell both have Sun in Taurus. Under pressure, Taureans will dig their heels in and refuse to budge. Rooted in nature, Taureans have the patience and determination to wait until they feel the time is right for them to act.

The Venus principle of Taurus is not about relationship per se, but about knowing what gives us pleasure and joy. I once worked psychotherapeutically with a Taurean client who was in an extremely depressed state. It turned out that he was living in a sixth floor flat with no contact at all to nature. Not only that, he was earning his money as a guinea pig for a pharmaceutical company testing medical drugs and working in a fast food hamburger outlet where the smell of the food disgusted him. The solution can often be very simple and tangible, and the first task I gave him was to buy some pot plants for his room and to take a daily walk in a nearby park. Eventually, as he learned to listen to his own senses, he moved out of London and went to live in the country. Venus is a powerful force and if she doesn't get what she needs then she will take her revenge on us. The natural balance of give and take will become distorted to all take and no give. An unfulfilled Venus will become extremely demanding to the point where she can manifest as all the seven deadly sins at once. She can become self-indulgent, greedy, lustful, jealous and covetous, which might express itself, for example, as a shopping addiction.

The integration of Mars, traditionally in its detriment in Taurus, will bring Venus and Mars into a positive relationship with each other, with Mars giving this sign the determination to stand up for its own values and to put itself and its own values first when necessary. The integration of the opposite sign of Scorpio will balance the emphasis on personal safety and security with a deep emotional connection to others and the courage to trust life.

Planets in Taurus
Audience: I have Moon in Taurus.

Clare: The Moon in Taurus tells us that what feeds and nourishes you, what makes you feel comfortable and secure, is plenty of contact with nature, an environment which is beautiful and peaceful, and the wherewithal to enjoy the simple, tangible pleasures of life. The Moon in Taurus resists change because it needs constancy and permanence, something to rely on. You may even need to eat your food slowly in order to savour the texture and taste. Imagine, for example, that your job involves constant travelling around the world. No matter how much you enjoyed your job, on an instinctual level you could begin to feel increasingly disorientated because Moon in Taurus needs to put down its roots in one place and stay there. Does this make sense to you?

Audience: Yes it does, but I also have several planets in fire signs.

Clare: That is interesting because it indicates that there is an inner conflict between two opposing elements. If these can be harnessed together, they will be extremely effective. What tends to happen, however, is that, because these elements appear to be mutually antithetical, we will suppress or project one of these elements and live out the other. Eventually, both the earth planets and the fire planets need to be acknowledged in their own terms and you will need to find space for each in your life.

Audience: Since joining this class I have felt my earth signs more strongly than my fire signs. I just feel very earthy in this group.

Clare: Is that a comfortable feeling, or does it make your fire go crazy?

Audience: No, but it certainly makes me dampen my fire. I feel less confident.

Clare: That must be quite uncomfortable?

Audience: Yes, definitely. On the other hand, I do feel very safe in this group.

Clare: It would be interesting to compare your chart with the group's chart to see what is happening. It may be that the group's Saturn sits on one of your fire planets or something like that. Each of us will respond to this group in different ways, depending on our own charts.

Audience: Didn't Jung have the Sun in Leo and the Moon in Taurus?

Clare: Yes, that's right, and he lived out both these elements very strongly. With the Sun in Leo his life was devoted to the search for meaning, through the exploration of mythology and symbolism. His goal, in his work with patients, was to encourage the development of 'consciousness', the journey of 'individuation' and the discovery of the 'Self', which are all very solar words. But on a personal level he found that working with his hands and working with stone was extremely healing. He had a real feeling for stones and rocks and the earth, and built his house at Bollingen with his own hands. He also needed to be a man of the soil.

Audience: I have Mars in Taurus.

Clare: Mars is traditionally in its detriment in Taurus. Here we have the planet of assertion, action and focus placed in the fixed Venus-ruled earth sign. How is Mars going to function in Taurus?

Audience: Slowly?

Clare: Yes, there is a determination and persistence and perseverance to Mars in Taurus, the ability to go on and on until you get to your goal. Mars in Taurus is practical, able to grapple with the real issues and achieve tangible results. At the end of the day, Mars in Taurus can move mountains. I believe there is a real strength to this placement, and a stubborn determination not to be deviated from one's course. Do you remember 'Swampy' at all?

Audience: Wasn't he the nature lover who lived in trees to stop people cutting them down, and then dug himself into tunnels under the earth to stop people clearing the land to build roads?

Clare: That's right. Swampy had Sun, Venus, Mars and Mercury in Taurus. He didn't collect petitions signed by thousands of people, which would be an air function, and he didn't stand on a soapbox and preach about the importance of nature conservation, which would be a fire function, and he didn't just feel miserable and upset about what was happening, which would be a water function. Instead, he just used his own body to obstruct the tree cutters and land clearers. This was a very strong statement which received a great deal of press coverage. It was not aggressive, because Taurus is a peaceful and gentle sign, but he was extremely persistent and, like all Taureans, he refused to budge until he was physically removed.

Let's have a look at Mercury in Taurus, which David has in his chart. This can be an indication of slow, methodical thinking and speaking and there is often a very beautiful and gentle voice, since Taurus rules the voice. Mercury in Taurus needs time to ground their ideas and time to make up their minds before they are prepared to speak. Once decided, however, Mercury in Taurus will stick to its ground.

Audience: I have Mercury in Taurus and I always need concrete proof before I will take anything on board. I am always searching for something solid to believe in. And I tend not to offer my opinions until I am sure of them.

Clare: It is often said that the earth signs are not comfortable with astrology, because it is such an abstract, mythic system, but a couple of years ago most of the students in my class were in fact Taureans, so I now know that is not true. I think astrology can be meaningful to the earth signs because it is rooted in history, with a strong foundation and tradition which has stood the test of time. The other reason is that I suspect that once the earth signs experience the fact that astrology actually works and that it can be immensely useful, then it has proved itself, which is good enough for them.

Sally has Chiron in Taurus which indicates that she may not feel inherently safe or secure or physically confident. We can anticipate that she will initially try to 'fix' this, as most of us do initially according to the placement of our own Chiron, by becoming extremely materialistic and possessive and by keeping tight control over her body and her money, her physical resources. The question with Taurus is usually about values, and with Chiron in Taurus Sally may be trying to gain security not according to her own values, but according to the values of others or of society. She can learn to accept and to trust her own instincts, no matter how unacceptable they may be to others, in the knowledge that 'the only difference between a flower and a weed is a judgment'.

VIRGO
Mutable Earth
Ruler: Mercury
Detriment: Jupiter
Fall: Venus

Virgo is a complex sign which takes some thinking about because, although it is an earth sign, it is also mutable and has Mercury as its ruler. The constellation of Virgo is that of the original archetypal great goddess before she was split into the many different aspects of the feminine. Ultimately the great goddess is virgin, which means self contained, 'complete and whole unto herself'. This is a description of mother earth, the feminine aspect of the life force itself, which doesn't need anything or anyone else to complete it. Another aspect of the feminine life force is Sophia, the archaic goddess of wisdom, who is said to have existed before the emergence of any male deities.

The Mercury ruler of Virgo describes the intelligent and analytical nature of this sign, but as an earth sign, this intelligence is used in a practical way, working with matter and substance in order to perfect and heal it. From this point of view, Virgo is concerned with the maintenance and perfection of the body, through diet, routine and healing practices. Equally, Virgo is the sign of all practical crafts devoted to creating something workable which is also useful, beautiful and refined. Virgo rules all rituals, and bringing to perfection the rituals of work and of the body are a feature of this sign. There is a strong mythic connection between the Mercury which rules Virgo and the god Thoth, the Egyptian Hermes, who taught all the practical skills and crafts to mankind, such as writing and medicine. Virgo is also the sign of the alchemist, whose task is to purify, refine and perfect base material.

Audience: Wasn't Thoth the scribe?

Clare: Yes. He was the inventor of language and of writing and functioned as the scribe, or record keeper of the gods. This is the difference between the Mercury which rules Gemini, which is the messenger of the gods, and the Mercury which rules Virgo, which is the scribe of the gods – a more earthy, practical figure. The function of record keeping gives us some important clues about Virgo. There is a sort of ritual about record keeping isn't there? It has a pleasure of its own. If you are wired in this particular way, the construction of neat columns of figures can be particularly satisfying, as can the feeling of creating order out of chaos, sorting the wheat from the chaff.

Virgos like things to be categorised and classified in an orderly way. They will usually have all their books in alphabetical order and know exactly where to find something in a drawer. Virgos are masters of practical common sense. Without this sign in the zodiac, there would be no order or attention to detail and none of us would be able to find anything. Virgo is modest and self effacing, at its best when it's being useful, attending to the small things of life. Virgos tend to have a horror of carelessness and crassness and a remarkable ability to spot an error or even a chip in a cup at 50 yards.

Audience: I can certainly relate to that.

Clare: I think the point is that Virgo can be really offended by imperfections, which they notice more than any other sign. They can also be more distressed by chaos and mess than other signs, which is what motivates them to sort and clean.

If we imagine the scene at a party to which fire and earth signs have been invited, it is likely to be the Virgos who are going round cleaning the ashtrays or in the kitchen washing up, while the fire signs are in full flow. Virgos are practical and like to be busy. They enjoy doing what needs to be done. They would often actually prefer to wash the glasses than to be fully involved in all the noise and confusion of the party itself.

Audience: I am a Virgo and I have never ever done that!

Clare: Well, naturally all these descriptions are just caricatures and nobody is all Virgo. And I think there are always plenty of Virgos who manifest the qualities of the opposite sign of mutable, watery Pisces. If this is the case, however, there is normally an element of anxiety which would not be present in a Piscean.

Audience: Aren't they very critical?

Clare: This is certainly one of the major features of this sign, but I think this is an extension of the fact that they are extremely self-critical. They expect nothing less than perfection of themselves, which tends to get extended towards criticism of others. If they can gain a sense of perspective, however, Virgos have a gentle, self-deprecating sense of humour, which makes them extremely amusing, pleasant company.. Physically Virgo rules the intestines, the function of which is to discriminate between what should be absorbed by the body and what should be eliminated. Virgos have very sensitive digestive systems and strongly psychosomatic constitutions. Everything needs to be carefully analysed, sorted and digested, and if they take on too much at once then they tend to become stressed and the body and digestive system will suffer. Virgos are prone to nervous exhaustion, and need to learn how to say no, how not to take on too much and how to establish healthy boundaries in order to protect themselves. They can be accused of being unfeeling and ungenerous, too workmanlike and 'cut and dried', but this can simply be an indication that they have learned to protect themselves from being overwhelmed.

The integration of Jupiter and Venus, traditionally in their detriment and fall in Virgo, can help to balance what can otherwise be an 'all work and no play' approach to life. Jupiter can keep the wood in mind as well as the trees, in other words help to put all the Virgoan attention to detail into a larger and more meaningful context. Venus can give permission to live simply and to enjoy the small details and rituals of life for their own sake, without the anxiety or stress which can so easily accompany such tasks.

Planets in Virgo
Audience: I have Moon in Virgo.

Clare: I would imagine that you really need to feel in control of your daily life and of your work?

Audience: Well I can certainly relate to a need for rituals. I always get very anxious and even quite obsessive when I break my normal routines, and that can extend to my diet as well.

Clare: David has both Uranus and Pluto in Virgo, which is a particularly interesting phenomenon shared by everyone born in the mid 1960s. With a few brief periods of retrogradation, Pluto was in Virgo for 15 years, from October 1956 to October 1971, and Uranus was in Virgo from August 1962 until September 1968, with the two planets closely conjunct during the mid 1960s. Uranus and Pluto form conjunctions every 125 years, and if we look back through history these are often periods of intense and radical collective change, the destruction of what has gone before and the birth of powerful new ideals. Radical thinkers whose ideas become very powerful and influential to later generations are often born at these times. However, the particular interpretation of each Uranus-Pluto conjunction will be different, since it depends upon the sign it falls in.

It is actually worth spending a bit of time on that Uranus-Pluto conjunction because I suppose it is the most powerful, radical generational influence around at the moment. What makes the picture more complicated is that those born in the mid 1960s also have Neptune in Scorpio, as well as Chiron and Saturn in Pisces, opposite the Uranus-Pluto conjunction. It would, of course, be quite possible to spend a whole term discussing this configuration, but for the time being we will just have to focus on Uranus and Pluto in Virgo. The point is that every generation in its own way breaks the old mould and brings in something new, which is taken for granted by subsequent generations.

If Virgo describes work, service and health, then we can anticipate that Pluto's transit through Virgo will intensify all these issues, bring any underlying problems to the surface, put them under great stress and change them forever. The simultaneous transit of Uranus through Virgo will bring radical change to these areas, innovations and breakthroughs. So we would expect the world of work and service and the area of health to go through a period of disruption and upheaval.

The 1960s has become famous as the decade of social and political upheaval. The civil rights movement was gaining strength, student demonstrations were taking place throughout Europe, the collective disillusionment with the Vietnam war was building and many former British colonies were establishing their independence. If you have a look at old film footage of these years you will easily be able to appreciate what a remarkably disruptive and radical period this was. J.F. Kennedy was assassinated in 1963, which was possibly the most shocking thing which had happened in American history until then. A technological revolution was occurring, with the development of the fibre optic cable and microchip which heralded enormous advances in computer technology, and the first telecommunications satellites which brought in instant communication across the world for the first time. In the world of health, the development of the contraceptive pill enabled women to be free of their biology and to have real control over their reproductive cycles for the first time in history. New technology was increasingly introduced to produce more crops and animals and to make them grow faster.

Audience: This is all very uncompromising, isn't it? I suppose that with Uranus and Pluto change is inevitable, but these changes seem to have had the effect of cutting us off even more from nature and from the natural cycles?

Clare: Yes, exactly. Uranus gives us sudden, radical freedom and of course there is no going back. This is a very far cry indeed from the concept of trusting nature to provide.

Audience: So this is actually a reversal, the destruction of Virgo in a way?

Clare: That's right. As a generalisation, we can describe the people born with this placement as intelligent, skilful, analytical and sensitive, and very modest on a personal level. There seems to have been a powerful evolutionary technological leap in the mid 1960s, which explains the fact that anyone born then and afterwards has an instinctive ability to understand and use technology in a way which is simply not possible for those born before this time. This generation tends to be collectively disgusted by the way things were managed before the 1960s, particularly in areas which concern work and the working environment as well as the unthinking destruction of the earth's natural resources. They are born to be radical, political and subversive, particularly when it comes to issues around food, health and ecology.

It is this group which has seen the destruction of our ties to nature and to work. They will never know 'cradle to the grave' employment as it used to be, as companies and organisations are streamlined and stripped down, becoming leaner and meaner. We can no longer rely on earning a crust or receiving our Virgoan daily bread. But equally, we could say that this is also a generation which has reacted against the old norms of work and service.

At the same time, Pluto and Uranus indicate that compensatory ideologies will be born. So this is a generation with strong ideals about work, health, ecology and the feminine. At worst, individuals from this generation can be cut off from an instinctive connection with their own bodies and become obsessed with diet and health issues, but because they have Uranus in Virgo they can simultaneously abuse their bodies. This sounds strange, but it is not uncommon for those with Uranus and Pluto in Virgo to be obsessed with health issues and at the same time starve themselves or abuse their bodies by taking drugs or not getting enough rest, in spite of having shelves full of books about eating right and cupboards full of supplements and vitamins. Or perhaps at the same time they will join radical and subversive movements and protest against, for example, animal experimentation, at the same time as treating their own animal bodies with a great deal of cruelty.

Audience: I can certainly recognise this. It's really tricky.

Clare: Exactly. Jung was very clear about the dangers of identifying with collective movements. We will inevitably resonate to them because they are in our charts, but unless we have a strong enough sense of self, we can easily become identified with them, which means that on a human level we will suffer. Provided we have a good enough ego structure, then we have a choice. We can always choose to serve the collective, but there is a great difference between a conscious choice and being possessed by an unconscious, archetypal force which means that our own lives will be sacrificed to a collective ideology.

CAPRICORN
Cardinal Earth
Ruler: Saturn
Exalted: Mars
Detriment: Moon
Fall: Jupiter

The sign of Capricorn begins at the winter solstice, the darkest time of the year. Capricorn understands the importance of the annual cycles and, as ruler of the coldest, darkest time of the year, is well aware of the necessity for stripping things back to their bare bones, cutting back and pruning, in order that they can grow stronger in the next season. Capricorn is the most mature of the earth signs and, as a cardinal earth sign, is goal oriented, ambitious and effective, with a strong sense of discipline and structure and the ability to plan ahead and wait for the right moment. Self sufficient and hardy, the mountain goat is an excellent symbol for this sign.

For Capricorn, time is the yardstick by which everything is measured. There is an ability to prepare, and to plan strategically, to accept responsibility and an ability to wait patiently for the fruit which will be the result of one's labours, with the knowledge that we will only reap what we have previously sown. For Capricorn, nothing is given for nothing and all things come to those that wait. Capricorn rules the body's structure and boundaries, the bones, skeleton and skin, as well as the knees, which are an interesting symbol of our flexibility and of our ability to 'bend the knee' to a higher authority. Deeply conservative, ambitious and cautious, this Saturn ruled sign has the determination and patience to take the hard and lonely road to the top, knowing that what it achieves has been hard won and truly deserved and can never be taken away.

The challenge for Capricorn is to integrate the determination and strength of the Saturn ruler and Mars exaltation with the gentle 'husbandry' of the opposite sign of Cancer and the caring nature of the Moon, in the knowledge that self discipline and patience will eventually bring things to their fruition. The positive integration of Jupiter in the sign of Capricorn indicates that, as in the case of many spiritual disciplines such as Tibetan Buddhism, for example, hard work and self discipline are well recognised paths of faith and dedication to a higher wisdom. Joy and satisfaction for Capricorn comes from knowing that we have conquered all obstacles and achieved our goals in spite of everything, and without having to depend on anything or anybody else.

Planets in Capricorn
David has the Moon in Capricorn, which is traditionally in its detriment here. With strong emotional (Moon) defences (Capricorn), Moon in Capricorn is self-sufficient (Capricorn) and may also need plenty of solitude (Capricorn). People with this placement are often more comfortable looking after others than being looked after themselves. It can describe a traditional (Capricorn) family (Moon), an older or professional (Capricorn) mother (Moon). Certainly this sign is not emotionally effusive or indulgent, and the early experience of mothering will reinforce this. There is often a preference for cold, dry food (Moon) which will be eaten slowly (Capricorn).

Audience: I have Venus in Capricorn.

Clare: Venus describes what we value, so I would suggest that you are likely to value (Venus) solitude (Capricorn), your social status and career (Capricorn), and perhaps your relationships (Venus) are chosen carefully (Capricorn). Venus in Capricorn values tradition and history and good quality – anything which has stood the test of time. These are the things which are likely to make you feel happy.

LESSON 10

The Air and Water Signs

The elements of air and water create our second pair of psychological opposites. In Wilber's quadrant system these two elements concern collective truth. For the air signs, the truth is objective, 'out there' in the systems created in the external world, and for the water signs, the truth is subjective, a connection to the emotional undercurrents and feelings which belong to us all, 'in here'.

The air signs of Gemini, Libra and Aquarius are the most civilized, most social, detached, abstract, rational and, in fact, the most 'human' of all the signs of the zodiac because they all concern the mind and the intellect. The word 'zodiac' means 'circle of animals', and yet the air signs are symbolized by human or abstract figures, with the twins representing Gemini, the scales of justice representing Libra and the figure of the water bearer representing Aquarius. The air signs describe the left and right brain functions, the capacity to think in opposites and to weigh up opposites – a duality which is symbolized by the Roman numeral II in Gemini, the two horizontal lines of Libra and the two wavy lines of Aquarius. The qualities of this element, which is positive and masculine, are valued in our culture and encouraged by our education system, which prizes and rewards the ability to think and communicate logically and rationally. Air signs are impersonal – they have the gift of detachment and objectivity and the gift of perspective. As signs of social interaction, they are articulate, natural negotiators, arbitrators and communicators, able to weigh up opposites and see both sides of the coin.

Audience: What's the shadow side of all that?

Clare: In general terms, we can say that the shadow for the air signs will be the element of water, the world of the emotions, which tend to be mysterious and rather murky, uncomfortable territory for air, since our emotions are so instinctive, subjective and non-verbal. Air signs tend to 'live in their heads' and are often out of touch with and embarrassed by emotions. In fact, they are often 'experts' when it comes to relationships. They can tell you a great deal about all the different theories of emotion and feelings, but this can often be a very clever defense against actually having to feel anything for themselves.

Audience: Presumably, it is not that the air signs can't feel – it is just that they can't express their feelings?

Clare: Yes, if you have enough planets in water then you will be in touch with the emotions and living with them all the time. If you don't have planets in water, the water function is still there, but is more likely to be operating autonomously, outside the control of the ego. So we are not saying: 'this person has no emotions', which is absolutely not true. The fact is that the emotions are very primal and autonomous and powerful because the person isn't working with them on a daily level. So when a mood comes over that person, it can be quite overwhelming.

For example, I once worked with a client who had very strong air and no water, who was having difficulty with a relationship. She would say things like, 'He has been seeing another woman, but I can quite understand and accept this because he is very emotionally needy and insecure and is afraid that if he loses me he will be alone'. This is a typical example of rationalization. It so happened that, owing to some powerful transits at the time, she found herself out in the street one night slashing the tires of her partner's car in an emotionally driven rage of revenge and pain which she was unable to relate to rationally or intellectually. This is an example of the water function taking its revenge on the control of the sophisticated, rational intellect. Once the feelings receded, and she was restored to her habitual rationality, my client was extremely embarrassed by her emotional outburst and said, 'I don't know what came over me'. This is exactly what it feels like when the shadow qualities are released; we are, literally 'beside ourselves'. So you can see that the air signs are likely to avoid emotional situations because they can so easily be taken over by them, and will run away if there is any danger of things getting messy because, by their very nature, emotions are messy and, according to air, irrational.

One of the main difficulties for people with a strongly developed air function is that, although they are extremely skillful at weighing up situations analytically, and can see both sides of the coin in any argument, they can end up feeling completely paralysed by the process. The fact that they know everything about a situation, all the pros and cons, and have looked at it from every side and read all the books about it doesn't help them decide what to do. This is the drawback of objectivity.

Audience: That's so true!

Clare: The point about the objective, exterior truth of the air function is that, although it can tell you all about something, it can't tell you the actual value of anything, which exists in other parts of ourselves, which the air function knows nothing about. It is the water function which tells us if something feels right or not, but this subjective emotional intelligence is something which, in our culture, we are often conditioned not to trust. For many people, learning to trust our subjective feelings and emotions can be one of the most important things we ever do.

Audience: My husband has many planets in air in his chart and he decided to buy a new computer. So he bought all the computer magazines and read up about all the options and investigated the whole subject for about six months, without making a decision. The strange thing about all this is that, eventually, he just went into the shop and bought the cheapest!

Clare: What an excellent example. First of all it sounds as if your husband approached the subject in a rational, intelligent way, analyzing all the pros and cons and, in fact, probably becoming an expert himself in the subject. However, none of this research told him what computer to buy – it just told him what was on the market and the various comparisons he could make. It sounds as if, at the moment he visited the shop, his feelings came to the surface, which were telling him that the computer wasn't emotionally important to him and therefore it wasn't worth spending more than necessary, something he obviously hadn't considered during his research phase!

The Air and Water Signs   177

The element of air in alchemy, portrayed in Michael Maier's *Atalanta fugiens* (1618). The caption for this image states: 'The wind has carried it in his belly.' This refers to air as the Mercurial *prima materia*, pregnant with the philosopher's stone or alchemical gold.

You see this phenomenon being played out on televised debate shows, with panels of people representing different views. No resolution or solution or progress emerges out of such debates, whose function seems to be mainly to clarify the opposing viewpoints, which is of value in itself but can easily go nowhere. There used to be a programme on the radio called *Moral Maze*, where a group of respected academics and intellectuals would sit around a table each week and discuss important moral issues. One week the panel was asked to debate the subject of whether or not the soul exists. The general consensus, of course, was that the soul did not exist because its existence had not been sufficiently proven according to the air signs' criteria of objective, collective truth. Another angle would be to suppose that the intellect can know nothing about the soul, and it is not uncommon for the air signs to talk about things they know nothing about.

The elements of earth and fire have their own ways of responding to the detached, objectivity of the air signs. The fire signs would get impatient and just leave air to carry on debating with itself, because fire is subjective and doesn't really care what other people think. Practical earth would not see the point of sitting around endlessly discussing concepts and theories. In fact, each element has its own particular way of thinking and acting and feeling.

Unlike the air signs, the water signs are non-verbal. The water signs tend to absorb the emotions and feelings behind what is being said, rather than the words themselves. Water is extremely sensitive to atmosphere, picking up subtle feelings about places and people which are strongly felt but not so easy to verbalise. Water is receptive, like a sponge, and able to empathise or 'feel with' others. With no inherent shape or form of its own, water takes on the form of its container. At best, water is simply supportive and non-judgmental. If you are upset or in pain, water can offer support, no matter what you have done or why you are feeling that way. For this reason, people often unburden themselves on water signs and cry on their shoulders, partly because, unlike air, they will not try and rationalize the problem away, which can be a way of ignoring and undervaluing the feelings.

Imagine, for example, that air and water go to a party together. As they walk into the room, air, who is interested in making social connections, might say: 'Great, there's so and so I know, there's so and so. I will introduce them to each other.' Water, on the other hand, might stand at the door and think: 'Hmm, this doesn't feel right. I'm not in the mood for this.' It this happens, then it doesn't matter who is in the room, they won't want to be there. Air and water have very different ways of processing information. Air will want to know what water's problem is and will ask for a rational explanation. At this point water feels overwhelmed because, as a mute, non-verbal element, it is difficult to put words to the feelings. Naturally, at this point, air begins to feels frustrated and irritated. Water then feels deeply misunderstood because it needs to have the problem intuited out of them, and might retaliate by saying something like: 'You don't understand me. You're so cold!' This will probably be interpreted as an irrelevant statement by air, whereas it was intended by water as a way to protect their inner feelings. These kinds of difficulties happen all the time because we don't understand

Johann Daniel Mylius, in *Philosophia reformata* (1622), portrays the element of water as protective and fecund. The dolphin, the creature of Apollo, rescues those who are in danger of drowning, while the woman on his back is the female Mercurius, the primal substance from which
the alchemical gold is made.

that other people process information and experiences in ways which are fundamentally different from us.

Audience: Can I go back to the missing element? My partner is very watery and she doesn't have a single personal planet in air. How does that work?

Clare: Well, we are talking about checks and balances here, and I think what tends to happen if the emotions are much stronger than the intellect, is that there is difficulty gaining any kind of detachment or perspective. This can result in a kind of emotional chaos, or getting waterlogged, like drowning in one's emotions, which can be very frightening. I expect that you may well have an emphasis of planets in air signs and not much water?

Audience: That's right.

Clare: So we can understand why you are together, because you will tend to hold the objective rational pole of the relationship and she may well carry the feelings for both of you.

GEMINI
Mutable Air
Ruler: Mercury
Detriment: Jupiter

Gemini is the child of the air signs, ruled by Mercury. Gemini is intelligent, curious, clever, witty and articulate, interested in everything, fascinated by information and facts and always learning. As a mutable air sign Gemini is particularly good at multi-tasking. The theme of duality runs right through this sign, and Geminis are often at their best when they are doing at least two things at once – such as reading a book while watching television, or checking their emails while talking to someone on the phone. This can also extend to other areas of life, since I have noticed that Geminis often buy two of this or that, and are immensely attracted to things that come in pairs, such as earrings and shoes!

As the butterfly of the zodiac, Gemini's strength is cross-fertilisation – making connections, putting different bits of information and different people together. Gemini rules the hands and the arms, and they tend to be dextrous and to 'speak' with their hands. Gemini also rules the lungs which deal with the taking in and giving out of air, or information. Gemini is a busy, active, light, youthful sign, and its mutability makes it very adaptable, flexible and changeable, with a mind like quicksilver and a real dread of being trapped or pinned down or of situations that might become 'heavy'. For example, if something more interesting comes along then, regardless of previous commitments they may have made, they are perfectly capable of changing their minds and going off in a different direction. Usually very articulate, fascinated by language itself, very good with words, Gemini doesn't want to take anything too seriously.

One of Gemini's particular gifts is the ability to act as a go-between or intermediary, and to break the tension of a difficult situation with a well timed joke or observation. Taxi drivers, couriers, people driving delivery vans and other people constantly on the move often have a strong Gemini emphasis in their charts.

Planets in Gemini
Audience: I have Moon in Gemini. What does that mean?

Clare: The Moon describes what feeds you, what makes you feel comfortable and safe, so we can suggest that it is information and communication that feeds you. You might feel very nourished, for example, by a good conversation. Meeting a friend for lunch, the exchange of information and the catching up with the gossip might feel more nourishing than the actual food you eat. On the other hand, you might even say to someone 'Leave me alone – I'm going to sit down and nurture myself by reading this newspaper or book', since the Moon is about the rituals which make us feel comfortable and about our instinctive, habitual needs. This also describes our maternal food, and perhaps a mother who was interested in teaching us or in feeding us with information. Moon in Gemini can also describe someone who has a real feel for languages. Freud is a good example of this. He was fascinated by language, the inventor of the 'talking cure' and the 'Freudian slip', the ways in which language reveals unintended messages.

Audience: Yes, I find I would much rather read a book than eat, although I will often do both at the same time, or grab something to eat when I am driving between appointments. Basically, I don't think I can relate to the emotions myself. I am much better at just relaying things to other people.

Audience: I have a compulsive need to assimilate information. Sometimes I hate this part of myself – it is almost like a bulimic tendency. I just can't stop.

Clare: So is your Moon connected to Mercury?

Audience: Yes, my Moon is in Virgo and makes a square to Mercury.

Clare: So we could say that there is a need for order and control, but Mercury's involvement could make you feel that you never have enough information to get it absolutely right? Your need to constantly assimilate more information could be an expression of a basic anxiety which, with Moon in Virgo, you might have absorbed from your mother.

Audience: Sally has Jupiter in Gemini. How do you think this will express itself in her life?

Audience: Well, if Jupiter expands what it touches, then I imagine this would be an extremely busy and active Jupiter indeed. In Gemini it could mean that Sally believes in words and in communication, and probably finds languages, and probably foreign languages too, very meaningful?

Clare: Absolutely. She could have a real aptitude, for example, in working as a simultaneous translator at conferences. Or she could be a very inspiring language teacher. The traditional detriment of Jupiter in Gemini indicates that she will need to be careful not to take on too much or to get over-stimulated or too scattered, which could result in an element of stress and nervous tension. Functioning positively, Jupiter can bring an overview, an appreciation of the whole picture, find a larger context for all the bits and pieces, and help Gemini develop a sense of trust and confidence.

Libra
Cardinal Air
Ruler: Venus
Exaltation: Saturn
Detriment: Mars
Fall: Sun

Libra is a cardinal air sign, which is important to remember because, as the Venus-ruled sign of one-to-one relationships, it is often automatically assumed to be a water sign. As a cardinal sign, Libra has very strong views about justice, harmony and civilized behaviour. Libra is refined – it rules all the civilized arts – the theatre, concert halls, art galleries, as well as the laws with which any civilized society conducts itself. Saturn, which is exalted in Libra, is very comfortable in this sign, since Saturn also rules laws. The function of Libra, as indicated by the symbol of the scales, is to balance the system.

Sometimes it is revealing to imagine what it would be like to completely remove a sign from the zodiac and to think about what would then be missing. Without Libra, for example, there would be no beautiful objects in our homes, no statues or gardens or parks in our cities, no graceful buildings or boulevards, no orderly queues, or manners or etiquette or polite consideration for others. All these Libran qualities are what make civilized life gracious and pleasant. Libran rules and laws and contracts make it possible for us to live together in harmony in the confidence that those who break the laws of civilized living will be justly punished. The Venus ruler of Libra is not the sensuous, physical, earthy Venus associated with Aphrodite. This Venus is more akin to Athena, the warrior goddess who was born from her father Zeus' forehead, fully grown and fully armed, with a sword in her hand. Her function was to protect heroes and brave warriors and to bring the arts of civilization to mankind. She is the patron of architecture and all the aesthetic arts.

There is a famous statue of Justice on the top of the Old Bailey in London, which I am sure you are familiar with. This female figure holds the sword of justice in one hand and the scales of justice in the other. In a sense she is an exact representation of the Aries-Libra axis in the birth chart. Libra is about aesthetics, about structure, style, grace, balance and harmony. As far as one-to-one relationships are concerned, Libra creates the contracts which define the agreed behaviour between two people, whether in business or personal relationships. Ideas and theories and concepts of peace and harmony and justice are Libra's strengths.

As a Venus-ruled sign, there is always something charming, graceful, pleasant and attractive about Librans, as well as a kind of androgenous quality. There is something rather feminine about the men and rather masculine about the women, which denotes an inner as well as outer balance. How things look and how people present themselves are important to Librans, and Libran taste and style can be relied on when it comes to interior decoration and fashion, since they have a sophisticated appreciation of balance and harmony. As intellectuals, it is likely to be the Librans at a ballet or concert who are following the score to ensure that the particular art form is performed correctly – the right way. Water and fire people, on the other hand, will simply be immersed in the emotional tension and drama, entering completely into the mythic or emotional experience.

It is genuinely important for Librans that the world and other people behave fairly, that 'justice is seen to be done' and that there is an equal balance of give and take in relationships. Librans believe strongly in contractual relationships, so that 'If I do this for you then you will do this for me' and 'If I am there for you, then you must be there for me'. There is always a *quid pro quo* where Libra is concerned: nothing is given unconditionally by Libra because this upsets the balance. But remember that this is not a water sign, and Libra gets very uncomfortable when emotional issues are stirred, because emotions tend to be uncivilized and messy and often unfair, which is not Libra's arena at all. From this point of view they can be very unrealistic about relationships.

Audience: But I thought they were romantics?

Clare: Oh yes, but as an air sign they tend to be in love with love as an art form or style. They want everything to be 'nice' – 'the whole nine yards', right down to the red roses, the candlelit dinners, words of love and soft music. A legal or marriage contract is a promise to behave in a certain way or to do a certain thing. There is nothing that upsets Librans more than when they feel they have been giving more than they receive, or if a contract has been broken. That is deeply, deeply upsetting and will normally trigger the surprisingly powerful and raw emotions which Librans normally try to avoid.

A good example of this is the film *The War of the Roses*, which some of you may have seen? The film begins with an extremely civilized, intelligent married couple, played by Michael Douglas and Kathleen Turner. They have a beautiful house and a manicured garden, the 'right' pictures on the wall, beautiful cars, they belong to the right social set and have respectable careers. In short, they have everything that the air signs could wish for. What they are not in control of, however, is their emotions, and the film is a terrifying tale of disintegration as the emotions take over and destroy everything they have created together.

Audience: Yes, I remember the terrible things they did to each other. It was a very disturbing film.

Clare: They ended up attacking each other with knives, running over each other's pets and generally behaving like crazed monsters. They are not at their best, Librans, in that kind of arena. They are very, very good when manners, diplomacy and charm are required. That's their best function. They are very skilled diplomats, excellent arbitrators, wonderful statesmen, and often have a tremendous gift for flattery. It is a kind of genuine looking for the best in others, so that they can be seen in the best light themselves.

Audience: Isn't this a bit harsh?

Clare: Well, you are right to point this out because, I know I have a Libran shadow! On the other hand, it is important to keep in mind that the qualities of the opposite sign are complementary and necessary for the full integration of each sign. In this case, Aries indicates that a strong sense of 'I' is essential if Libra is to function positively. As an air sign, Libra often doesn't understand that problems cannot be solved by the rational intellect alone. Shaking hands after a dispute attends to the form but does nothing to resolve the emotional undercurrent of the problem. The concept of 'peace talks' is a good example of this. The intention is to bring in rational detachment to solve a problem which often has very deep emotional roots, to put the problem on the table and look at it in a detached way in order to negotiate a compromise. Does this make sense to you? Obviously *The War of the Roses* resonated?

Audience: I am a Libran myself, and it was so horrible when I broke up with my ex-husband – exactly like the film!

Clare: What is so interesting when contracts are broken or ended, such as in divorce, is that on one level this is dealt with in a very civilized way through lawyers and through the law courts. This is where a pre-nuptial contract comes into its own, and indeed it must have been a Libran who invented these in the first place! It is a well known fact that Michael Douglas and Catherine Zeta-Jones signed a prenuptial contract and that they share the same birthday – 25th September – so they are both Librans! Catherine Zeta-Jones also starred in a film called *Intolerable Cruelty* with George Clooney starring as a society divorce lawyer. This was another excellent exploration of the contractual side of marriage, which hinged entirely around the subject of pre-nuptial agreements. The film was a good portrayal of the fact that no 'negotiated settlement', legal separation or divorce can help with the emotions or feelings which underlie such situations.

Moving on – has anyone got any planets in Libra that they would like to look at?

Planets in Libra
Audience: I have Mars in Libra.

Clare: Mars describes how you defend and assert yourself, how you fight. With Mars in Libra I suspect that you find it easier to fight for others than for yourself if you feel an injustice has been done? This indicates that you are probably a natural mediator and arbitrator, and you will feel comfortable in these kinds of situations. It is harder for Mars in Libra to stand up for themselves since they often intellectualise the problem and can easily find reasons why the other person is behaving in a particular way, arguing against themselves, if you like. On the other hand, this placement describes a 'just war'. If a contract has been broken, an injustice done, this can spur the Libran on towards righting the wrong, although this will normally be done with great style. Do you find that injustices will really get you going?

Audience: Absolutely.

Clare: Sally has Pluto in Libra, which is a collective placement well worth looking at. Pluto was in Libra from 1971 to 1983 which indicates that the collective corruption and decay which is ready to be brought to the surface, purged and eliminated will concern issues of equality, fairness, justice and trust. The Watergate affair of 1972 and 1973 in the US is one example. We could say that, until this time, it was collectively assumed that people in positions of power would behave in a generally ethical, legal and honourable way, and that the legal system could be more or less trusted to deliver justice. Now that Pluto has been through Libra, I think we are all much more aware of the corruption which exists under the surface in big organizations. But at the time, the Watergate affair was particularly shocking because on a collective level we still expected people in positions of authority and responsibility to behave ethically.

On a personal level, the burning ground for this generation will hinge around issues of trust and personal responsibility in relationships, which are likely to go through periods of breakdown and re-creation as those with Pluto in Libra struggle to find more honest, balanced and integrated ways to manage their relationships. This is very different indeed to the Neptune in Libra generation born between 1942 and 1956. This was a generation whose collective dream and longing was for peace, love and harmony. This was the hippy generation which idealized relationships and believed, in the immortal words of John Lennon, who also had Neptune in Libra, that 'All you need is love'.

Audience: So, with Pluto in Sagittarius at the moment, what is the corruption which is coming to the surface?

Clare: Sagittarius concerns higher education, the church and the law, and I think it is true to say that all these areas are currently under severe pressure to get their respective houses in order. In the UK universities are now meant to be available to all, and no longer places of privilege. However, this has meant that student grants have been replaced by loans, and universities are now under extreme financial pressure to survive at all. In the church there continue to be enormous struggles over the question of the ordination of gay priests and women bishops, not to mention the exposure of priests who have molested children. In Sagittarian terms, as God's representatives priests, are not supposed to be bodily motivated at all, but all these issues have come to light since Pluto entered Sagittarius. In the legal world, the corruption of the Legal Aid system has now been exposed. Pluto adds fanaticism and obsession, which could describe the current growth of fundamentalism and the rise of religious cults.

AQUARIUS
Fixed Air
Traditional Ruler: Saturn
Collective ruler: Uranus
Detriment ruler: Sun

It is difficult to visualise fixed air, except symbolically as fixed ideas and ideals or, perhaps, as the structured intellect or rigid thinking. What we can certainly say is that when we look at the sign of Aquarius we are once again reminded of the duality of the air signs generally and immediately confronted with a sign which contains radical contradictions, described by the very different motivations of the two planetary rulers of this sign: Saturn and Uranus.

Saturn and Uranus are opposites in almost every sense. Saturn stands for tradition, structure, order, hierarchy, authority and the status quo. Uranus stands for the force which seeks to break down the status quo and the old structures which Saturn seeks to preserve. Uranus is an innovator – the carrier of new ideals for the benefit of the collective. Uranian ideals are utopian to the extent that they concern openness and honesty, democracy and equality, and the possibility of humanity raising itself to a level where we can respect each other's differences and work together for the greater good of all.

Aquarius is the most civilized, developed, humanitarian and mature of the air signs. It concerns social structures and organizations and political systems whose goal is to help society advance and improve the condition of ordinary people. It is humanitarian, socially opinionated. The Saturn ruler describes the social structures and the Uranus ruler gives this sign an extra charge because of its foresight, ideals and sense of the future possibilities for the perfection of humanity. Can you see how both these planets, in spite of their radical differences, can be associated with this sign? The integration of the Sun, which is in its detriment in Aquarius, can be an important clue to the fully mature expression of this sign. As the planet of individuality, the Sun indicates that, ideally, individual values and personal self expression will balance the collective concerns of this sign.

Planets in Aquarius
Audience: I have the Sun in Aquarius.

Clare: Do you feel you are in touch with some kind of knowledge or foresight or vision which would be useful to mankind?

Audience: Well, I certainly have an unconventional way of seeing the world. I tend to think in an entirely different way from other people.

Clare: Yes. Aquarians have a tendency to turn things on their head, to come at things from a different perspective than the norm, to think 'outside the box'. Would you say in your experience you feel both your Saturn ruler, which makes it important for you to achieve respect in the community or in the group, and also this extra something that makes you different, that wants to challenge the group, break down the old structures and replace them with something better?

Audience: Funny you should say this, but this is exactly how I feel.

Clare: I think it is important for Aquarians to come to terms with this paradox because the sign is inherently opposed to itself. Saturn, for example, cares what other people think, and Uranus doesn't give a damn. This is where the famous Aquarian phrase comes from: 'I love humanity, it's people I can't stand'. In spite of its inherent contradictions, the fixity of Aquarius describes its tremendous loyalty and its high ideals of friendship. There is a real clarity and detached honesty and truthfulness and open friendliness about this sign, and nothing which is gooey or mushy. Those of us who have Aquarian friends can count ourselves as very fortunate.

There is often a tremendous sense of liberation for Aquarians when they get to the point of not caring what other people think, because they have always been and always will feel different from the norm. When we are young, this can be extremely uncomfortable and many Aquarians spend a great deal of energy trying to 'join the herd' by behaving and dressing like everyone else in order to cover up this sense of separateness. Saturn's influence in the first half of life brings a sense of inadequacy and a fear of being exposed or ridiculed in any way. As the Uranus ruler of this sign becomes stronger, people with an emphasis of planets in Aquarius tend to become more and more comfortable being who they are and start to enjoy deviating from the norm.

Audience: This is very helpful, because as an Aquarian I have always felt very different, but at my Saturn return I stopped minding and started to enjoy it.

Clare: Yes, it seems that by the time of your first Saturn return you had earned the experience and self knowledge to give yourself permission to be different.

Audience: Yes, it was very reassuring. Until then I didn't feel as if I was being truthful to myself, which is difficult for an Aquarian.

Audience: What about the Aquarian shadow? How does that work?

Clare: If we approach this from the point of view of water being opposite to air, the shadow side of Aquarius can be described as an undervaluation of ordinary human feelings and emotions. There is a kind of ideological rigidity or totalitarianism to Aquarius which can be autocratic, uncompromising and brutal to the extent that it rides roughshod over ordinary human concerns. With their inherent sense of superiority, Aquarians can be critical of ordinary mortals, who can be too slow or flawed or stupid to appreciate their brilliance, truth and clarity.

Audience: And when the world eventually catches up, the Aquarian has moved on to the next vision.

Audience: I don't know if this is significant, but my Moon is in Leo and my Sun is in the opposite sign of Aquarius.

Clare: So what we need to be looking at a great deal in your particular chart is the Aquarius-Leo polarity and the importance of integrating this polarity. You were born around the time of a full Moon, when the Sun and Moon are as far apart from each other as they get. This means that you have this polar opposite within, which will give you maximum objectivity about these two principles in your chart. The task is to find out what they mean as separate principles and then to integrate them, because we need to integrate the opposites if we are not to be pulled apart by them. We will be looking at all this in much more detail next term.

Audience: I have Moon in Aquarius, but surely this is a contradiction in terms, because the Moon is about the emotions and about neediness and is watery, but Aquarius is about detachment and ideas?

Clare: The Moon simply describes what you need in order to feel comfortable and nurtured and safe. Moon in Aquarius actually needs space and detachment, honesty, loyalty, truth and equality in friendships. It is ideas and ideals which will feed you. The lunar bond is created with people with whom we share like minds. This is just as strong a need as anything watery. People with an Aquarius Moon often have the feeling that they have been born into a family with whom they have nothing in common: 'Who are these strangers?' It can also indicate that your mother doesn't fit the normal 'mothering role', but is unusual in some way, perhaps a woman ahead of her time, someone who is more comfortable being your equal and your friend now that you are grown up, than she was when you were a baby.

Sally has Sun, Venus and Mercury in Aquarius. Mercury in Aquarius indicates that she is likely to be intelligent, rational and detached, fair minded and logical. Her thinking will be structured and scientific in its approach and she will expect others to be her intellectual equals and to hold the same ideals that she does. Venus in Aquarius indicates that she values honesty, truth and loyalty and will be an extremely loyal friend. The Sun indicates that she will identify strongly with her values and with her ideals. This is a very highly principled, possibly autocratic, unyielding combination. The integration of the opposite sign of Leo and of its ruler, the Sun, will help her develop an appreciation of the importance of unique individual values in the implementation of collective ideals.

David, on the other hand, has Saturn in Aquarius. This is a more cautious placement and indicates that he may be very sensitive to being judged by others or being thought to be stupid. He will tend to look to authority figures for the answers and seek to conform to collective norms and expectations in order to avoid being exposed or excluded. Eventually, he will develop his own knowledge and expertise and become an authority on his own terms. He has a disciplined and structured mind and this placement is often found in the charts of scientists and strategists.

Audience: I have Chiron in Aquarius.

Clare: Yes, how many people have this placement? Three or four of you. This is really an extension of what we have been talking about. Chiron is the outsider, the maverick, the one that doesn't belong and is therefore often scapegoated by the group. Chiron in Aquarius, the sign of the group, often describes a person who has made many attempts to be accepted by others and has had many painful experiences of being the one that didn't fit, the one that was picked on, excluded and rejected by the group. This can lead to a wounded rejection of any collective situations, the rationalization that 'I never wanted to join anyway' which can in fact be simply a defense against being rejected again. So the wound of Chiron in Aquarius is about being isolated from or rejected by the group. Eventually, rather than cutting ourselves off altogether, we can come to accept ourselves just as we are, without needing the permission or even the understanding of others. It is not unusual for astrologers, for example, to find themselves at the receiving end of the judgements and criticisms of 'normal' people because we have a particular way of thinking which is not shared by the collective. However, when we find ourselves in a group of other astrologer mavericks then we can all be outsiders together, which is very comforting, and once we have accepted ourselves just as we are, then we no longer have to fight to be accepted by others.

Audience: But surely, in the end, the eventual outcome is that there is a collective moving forward which gradually brings more knowledge and clarity?

Clare: Yes, I think we would all like to believe that this is true. There is no doubt that there has been an exponential increase in scientific discoveries and inventions since the discovery of Uranus, which does indicate a collective leap, a new kind of collective intellectual capacity with which to address and resolve our problems. What seems to be hanging in the balance, however, is whether we can harness our undoubted potential with real wisdom and compassion.

Let's try and get into some water now. We need to plunge down from the clear, distant, rarified heights of Aquarius, into the murky depths of water, where we are dealing with a much more mysterious and archaic world.

CANCER
Cardinal Water
Ruler: Moon
Exalted: Jupiter
Detriment: Saturn
Fall: Mars

As a cardinal water sign, a useful image for Cancer is water moving powerfully in one direction or another, such as rivers and waterfalls and waves. I think the key to this sign is its tidal nature, since it is ruled by the Moon, which is constantly waxing or waning and rules the ebb and flow of the tides. Physically, Cancer rules the breasts and the stomach, the functions of giving out nourishment to others and taking in nourishment for oneself. For so long as the ebb and flow are kept in some kind of balance, this sign tends to function positively.

When the tide is coming in, Cancerians can be sociable, generous and loving, crazy, lunatic and exuberant. When the tide is going out the Cancerian will retreat and you will get nothing but the shell. You can knock on the shell but there is nobody there. In common with all the water signs, there is something very private about this sign. Cancerians will hide under rocks and not respond, except under duress, when they are likely to be extremely crabby and touchy. The Cancerian Marcel Proust, whose life can be described as falling into two major tides, spent the first half of his life as a socialite, and the second half of his life as a recluse in a padded apartment in Paris, during which time he wrote his famous book *Remebrance of Things Past* which is full of references to his mother and to memories of food. This is an extremely sensitive sign with strong emotional connections to the past, not just the personal past but an interest in the origins and roots of all things. Cancerians can do nostalgia better than any other sign.

It is not unusual for Cancerians to get stuck at one extreme end of the spectrum. At the all-nurturing, all-giving, all-providing, all-self sacrificing end of this tidal spectrum, there is often a shadow side which is full of resentment and self pity. Alternatively, the all-demanding, dependent, needy, vulnerable end of the spectrum is too much for most people to cope with, which will reinforce the sense of abandonment and dependency and the Cancerian will become even more emotionally demanding and clingy. Cancerians can also be very manipulative and masters of emotional blackmail along the lines of 'If you don't eat my food it means you don't love me'.

The positive integration of Saturn and Mars, which are in their detriment and fall in Cancer, can help the Cancerian to develop the strength to stand on their own feet (Saturn) and to stand up for themselves (Mars). As a cardinal sign, Cancer is extremely tenacious and determined and, like a crab, tends to approach its goals subtly and invisibly and, when nobody else is looking, get what it wants to the surprise of all.

Audience: What is the meaning of the Jupiter exaltation in Cancer?

Clare: Ultimately, the sense of belonging, which is such a feature of this sign, reaches beyond the personal clan to greater connections to community, society, country, to ancestors and back into history. Water is impersonal, it is just as likely, and a great deal safer, for a Cancerian to draw its strength from a deep emotional connection to mother earth herself. Jupiter expands, and in this sense Cancerians can often find meaning through a sense of belonging to something which is much larger than the personal family.

Audience: My son is a Cancerian and I never feel that I really know him. I can never get to his centre.

Clare: It sounds as if you are trying to prize his shell open, which is unlikely to succeed. Cancer is immensely protective and self protective.

The strength of this cardinal water sign is that it achieves its goals quietly and subtly. It is prepared to wait for the tide, or until everybody else has lost interest. I suspect that your son doesn't want you to penetrate into his soft centre, which he will only reveal in his own time and on his own terms. Most of the time he is likely to throw up smoke screens as a way of defending himself.

Audience: But why won't he ever give me a straight answer to a straight question?

Clare: Do you, by any chance, have a strong air emphasis in your chart? Yes, I thought so. This is a good example of the tension between the opposite elements of air and water. You won't get a straight answer because your son is a water sign. You will get deflection, deviation and changing the subject and you will get a lot of other stuff but what is really happening is you are not getting the answer. This is not accidental, but an example of a watery defensive mechanism working powerfully.

Audience: I thought that Cancerians were very trusting?

Clare: I don't think so. My feeling is that this sign naturally tends not to trust unless it is absolutely safe to do so. On the other hand it is normally safe to trust the past and to trust memories.

Planets in Cancer

Sally has Mars in Cancer, so this will describe how she asserts and defends herself. This is an extremely self-protective placement, and Sally is likely to protect her own feelings very strongly. Although this planet is traditionally in its fall in Cancer, it also describes the kind of fierce aggression with which a mother will protect her young. She is perfectly prepared to fight to the death to protect them. If we can find the right relationship to this placement of Mars, there is nothing weak about it at all.

Audience: I have Uranus in Cancer, and I have certainly rebelled against my family and even against my country, since I left the US when I was 18. As soon as I could, basically.

Clare: Yes, that is an excellent example of a generational issue. Uranus was in Cancer from June 1949 until August 1955, with a brief period back in Cancer between January and June 1956. A kind of shorthand for Uranus in the chart is to ask 'what is it that we don't believe in?', 'where do we feel cut off?'. Uranus in Cancer refers to a particular group of people who, in general terms, don't believe in family, in belonging or in any kind of biological containment. Any kind of nest will make Uranus in Cancer panic. Many people with Uranus in Cancer actually dislike their relatives and simply don't want to be involved. They will leave home or travel to another country as soon as possible.

The Uranus in Cancer generation often feel like strangers in their own family or in their own culture, and the urge will be to challenge the status quo or to escape. There is a kind of double bind to this. On the one hand, as a generation there is an urge to break down the old patterns and habits, rebel against the restrictions and limitations of family and culture and seek to find new ways to belong which are not genetically or historically programmed. This generation will seek to make new connections based on intellectual honesty and shared minds and new ways of living. The Uranus in Cancer generation, for example, has tended to reject the values and religious traditions of their own cultures, finding it much easier to adopt the religious and philosophical traditions of cultures other than their own. Before 1949 we could even say that the 'nuclear family' was the rock upon which societies and cultures were built, and that it was not until Uranus entered Cancer that this began to be challenged. Nowadays, of course, we take the fragmentation and breakdown of the family unit for granted and one parent families are now the norm.

On the other hand, from a personal point of view this fragmentation can be immensely painful because, as ordinary human beings, it is hard for us to feel alienated from our biological and cultural roots. Taken to extremes, this placement can lead to a refusal to belong to any group at all or, as Groucho Marx famously remarked, to any club which will have us as a member, which means that we can be in a state of rejection and refusal which traps us just as much as being caught within a family clan. This is an example of the way our Uranian ideology can trap and imprison us. We can find ourselves rebelling against and pushing away any intimacy and containment which, on one level, is anathema to us but which, on an ordinary, human, lunar level we desperately need. If there are other planets in Cancer as well as Uranus, then a tension is set up because you are part of a generation that wants to destroy the very thing you need on a personal level.

The point I am trying to make here is that, unless we can make some kind of conscious relationship to the generational issues we are all born into, then we are at their mercy. At its most dangerous, Uranus is 'group think', blind, collective ideology. This can result in an identification with some kind of external ideology which has never been taken down in voltage, internalized or brought down to a human scale. We need a strong ego structure in order to find our own relationship to the collective forces if we are not to be possessed by them.

Audience: I have Uranus in Cancer and as soon as I went to university my parents sold the family house and moved to the other side of the country. I found that devastating.

Audience: I find that as I get older my family gets more important.

Clare: Perhaps at last, now that you have a strong enough sense of yourself and a good strong ego structure, it is safe to get closer to them without being overwhelmed? There is no doubt that with Uranus in Cancer you can be the positive carrier of necessary change and honest truthfulness which your family can benefit from considerably.

Audience: Does that mean that the current generation who are being born with Uranus in Aquarius will be against ideologies?

Clare: Well that would be a logical assumption, but I suppose we will have to wait and see.

SCORPIO
Fixed Water
Personal Ruler: Mars
Transpersonal Ruler: Pluto
Detriment: Venus
Fall: Moon

As a fixed water sign, Scorpio is like a very deep, dark, still well. The phrase 'still water runs deep' is particularly appropriate here because although the surface of the water may be calm, there is always a strong sense of the mysterious and unknown and often frightening depths lying below the surface. At the bottom of the well lies rotten, decayed and decaying detritus which all of us, unless we are Scorpios, would rather not think about. There is an intense magnetism about Scorpio and people tend to be either strongly attracted or strongly repelled by its atmosphere of inscrutability and controlled power. As a water sign, this magnetism is generated by a powerful emotional intensity which Scorpios will bring with them when they walk into a room, creating a change or a shift in the atmosphere. Can you relate to this?

Certainly, there is nothing superficial about this sign, and Scorpios never take life lightly. This sign does not share the tidal nature of Cancer or the fluidity of Pisces. Its stillness, darkness and depth make it the most emotionally intense sign of the zodiac. This is a sign of extremes, ice or fire, black or white, never anything in between, and there is often a kind of obsessive intensity which can be either very destructive or immensely creative. Normally secretive, private and controlled, Scorpios, like volcanoes, will either be dormant or active. It is unlikely that you will ever get anything at all out of a dormant Scorpio – there is an impenetrability and a stillness, and even Scorpio eyes will give nothing at all away. This does not mean, of course, that nothing is happening below the surface. Quite the opposite. Scorpios are processing emotions all the time, and storing up impressions and experiences which will be used later. As a very controlled sign, Scorpio can afford to wait. Scorpio has a prodigious memory, a penetrating mind and a compulsion to probe under the surface. Detectives, depth psychologists, doctors and even potholers, and people working in submarines, 'under the surface', often have an emphasis of planets in Scorpio.

You will be in no doubt at all when you meet a Scorpio in its active volcano phase. Scorpios are often accused of stirring up trouble, being paranoid and suspicious and smelling rats where there are no rats. Although this may be true, it is also true to say that Scorpios have very keen noses and if they sense that something is being hidden which has become poisonous, or if something has become emotionally polluted or distorted, then they will feel compelled to bring it to the surface in order that it can be eliminated so that the system or organism as a whole can be purged, cleansed and healed. As with all the water signs, Scorpio is, ultimately, an impersonal force. This explains why Scorpio is the sign of the healer and there is no doubt that Scorpios tend to function as agents of purging, not only on a personal level but, as the ruler Pluto indicates, on a collective level as well. Scorpios are often blamed for this compulsion to bring issues which are hidden, taboo or poisonous to the surface so that they can be healed.

There are various creatures associated with this sign, one of which is the serpent which renews and regenerates itself by shedding its old skins on a regular basis. Scorpios often seem to go through several lifetimes within one life. Each 'death' will be experienced as a period of crisis, during which anything which has been outgrown is eliminated, followed by the generation of a completely new chapter in life. If you are living with Scorpio planets or a Scorpio Ascendant, life is not a game. It is an intense struggle for survival, about constantly having to go into the fires to be reborn. The mythic phoenix is also associated with this sign, the bird which periodically enters into a fire, burns itself up and regenerates itself once again. There is also the actual scorpion level, of course. Solitary creatures with poisonous stings which live in the desert and in dry, barren wastes and which we will do well to treat with great caution and circumspection. Finally, there is the eagle, which symbolizes the scorpion nature which soars above the world, having completely transformed and purified itself and, no longer caught by emotional complexities or defensiveness, has become magnificently itself.

Audience: So they are always purging themselves? Would you say that Scorpios live several lifetimes in one life?

Clare: Exactly. The other interesting thing about Scorpio is that the birth process itself is often a real struggle for survival.

Audience: I have Scorpio on the Ascendant, and I nearly died in the process of being born.

Clare: It is not unusual to hear people with Scorpio on the Ascendant say this. And, although we will explore the meaning of the Ascendant in much more depth next term, in astrological terms the way we enter life is also the way we live our lives. This means that your sensitivity to personal danger and your struggle for survival will probably be a general theme in your life.

Audience: So Scorpio Ascendant can be quite difficult?

Clare: Difficulty is not exclusive to the sign of Scorpio, but we can certainly say that for people with a Scorpio Ascendant, life is not a bed of roses but something which is met with great intensity, strength and depth of feeling. It is often said, for example, that when a Scorpio is born, someone in the family has just died or is about to die. Equally, when a Scorpio dies, there is a birth in the family. There is something deeply archaic and organic about all the water signs, connected to hidden laws of life and death. Scorpio is about getting to the heart of the emotional truth, which can manifest as a brutal honesty which is too much for many of us. If you don't want to know the truth, then don't ask a Scorpio!

The Mars ruler of Scorpio is not the rash, headstrong Mars which rules Aries. This Mars is controlled and subtle, the professional soldier rather than the football hooligan, the knife used with skill and precision by the surgeon, rather than the knife used by a robber in the heat of the moment. The Pluto ruler of Scorpio refers to the purging of that which has become polluted, poisonous or taboo in the collective. In the same way, Scorpio rules the organs of elimination in the body, and elimination is absolutely essential if the body is not to become poisoned. The conscious integration of Venus and the Moon, the feminine planets of gentleness, peace and caring which are in their detriment and fall in

Scorpio, can soften the otherwise brutal effectiveness of this sign and help it to take the values and needs of others into consideration.

Audience: My sister has five planets in Scorpio and a friend of mine won't even talk to her. But you can trust her with anything and you can tell her anything. She is tremendously loyal. She keeps her feelings to herself, but I have learned never to ask for her opinion unless I am feeling strong enough to take it.

Clare: And I am sure that your secrets are safe with her? This loyalty is a feature of all the fixed signs and Scorpio is extremely loyal to its own feelings and to the feelings of others. There is a tremendous strength to this sign, and you can be sure that no crisis or emotional turmoil will be too much for them to cope with. Indeed, these sorts of situations are when Scorpios come into their own. Once you have earned the loyalty of a Scorpio, they will go through heaven and earth, ice and fire for you.

It is interesting that images of hell and of the underworld, which are familiar landscapes for Scorpio, contain both images of ice and fire, frozen lakes and eternal fires. On the other hand, if you betray the trust of a Scorpio then you are going to be in trouble. Scorpios invented the phrase 'Revenge is a dish best served cold'. And if you attack a Scorpio you will feel the sting, which is, in fact, a defensive mechanism. This is why the sign has a bad name, of course. It is said to be a sign of vengeance but, strictly speaking, if you leave a scorpion alone you will be safe.

Audience: Are there any other levels?

Clare: There is a particularly appropriate example in the Dumas story of *The Count of Monte Cristo*. In this story, Edmund Dantes, who is our Scorpio man, is imprisoned for a crime he didn't commit and his wife married the man who had unjustly imprisoned him. Dantes finally escaped after 30 or so years in prison and, because Scorpios never forget any wrongs done to them, systematically went about getting his revenge. He took the wrong-doer to pieces, bit by bit, in a very precise, calculated and extremely deadly way; that was the retribution.

At root, Scorpios have healing power. They can make themselves ill and they can also heal themselves. If they can find the right relationship to the Pluto ruler of this sign, they can function as channels of the collective life force itself, able to heal others. There are many Scorpio doctors, and of course you have to be very strong indeed to be a channel for the healing power of nature, and you will need to have been in the depths yourself to truly understand that this force cannot be harnessed to the ego's will without it causing great damage to the individual. Water supports, cleanses and heals, and it is not unusual for a Scorpio to be born with the task of carrying, bearing, suffering and finally purging deep ancestral or collective poisons for which they will often be blamed and for which they will certainly receive no thanks.

Planets in Scorpio
Both our case studies have generational planets in this sign. David has Uranus in Scorpio and Sally has Neptune in Scorpio. Uranus was in Scorpio from November 1974 to November 1981, with a brief retrograde period back into Libra from May to September 1975. Anyone born during this time will seek to gain clarity and detachment from the murky undercurrents of this deeply emotional sign. There may be a refusal to be pulled down into complex relationships and a determination to resolve old issues and purge past wrongs by bringing them under the light of the intellect. The Uranus in Scorpio generation will act as a radical new broom in this cupboard, bringing a new and more idealistic approach to understanding relationships and issues to do with joint finances. For example, there may be a reaction against any shared resources and a determination not to rely emotionally on anyone else. On a personal level, this can lead to an inability to really trust others and to explosive and disruptive relationships. The individual may cut themselves off altogether if relationships become too emotionally complex or demanding. Neptune was in Scorpio from October 1956 to November 1970, with a brief period of retrogradation in Libra from June to August 1957.

If Neptune describes where we are always thirsty and where we long to surrender, this placement can be described as Dionysian, an intense and even obsessive longing for powerful, dark and dangerous collective experiences which break down the sense of isolation and lead to emotional catharsis and a feeling of emotional rebirth. The popularity of 'raves' and their association with the drug ecstasy has plummeted this generation into scenes which are pure re-enactions of the drug and alcohol fueled orgies dedicated to Dionysus in ancient Greece! Naturally, not everyone born with Neptune in Scorpio will be addicted to drugs or group catharsis, but on some level the longing for intense emotional surrender will find expression in one way or another. On a personal level, this placement is likely to find expression in personal relationships, and there can be an intense longing for deep emotional connection, difficulty establishing healthy boundaries, emotional confusion and dissatisfaction as the individual comes under the grip of this powerful collective placement.

PISCES
Mutable Water
Personal Ruler: Jupiter
Transpersonal Ruler: Neptune
Exaltation: Venus
Detriment: Mercury

I have nothing to say about Pisces, so we can all go home now! The problem is that the sign of Pisces is so inclusive that it is very difficult to define, or to get any kind of intellectual grip on it. As the most mature water sign, Pisces is also the most collective, non-personal sign of the zodiac. In this sense, Pisces can be whatever you want it to be since, as a mutable water sign, it is the chameleon of the zodiac, taking on the shape and colour of its environment. The Jupiter ruler of Pisces describes the potentially joyful, ecstatic 'dolphin' nature of this sign. Pisces has a heightened sensitivity to beauty and can enter realms of fantasy and imagination which other signs can only dream of. Pisceans are often masters of creative self expression, wonderful actors, since they can feel their way into any persona, and often tremendously skilled in non-verbal communication, such as dance, art and music, capable of merging and surrendering to forces and feelings which are greater than themselves.

Planets in Pisces are like psychic sponges. For example, if a person who is depressed or angry or unhappy walks into a room, the Piscean can easily begin to feel depressed or angry or unhappy themselves, without knowing why. If this capacity for symbiotic merging is consciously recognized and harnessed, it can be an extremely useful gift for anyone working in the helping and healing professions. Pisces has an immense capacity for non judgmental compassion and unconditional devotion which can be directed towards anything or anyone who is suffering or in need. However, unless this sensitivity is to some extent defined and contained, Pisceans can all too easily find themselves overwhelmed by the emotions of others or by the environment in which they find themselves, leaving them adrift and at the mercy of others and of the world.

This capacity for total immersion and absorption also crosses the boundaries of space and time. It is not unusual for Pisceans to become mediums or channels, or to discover that they are psychically connected

The two fish of Pisces portrayed in Lambsprinck's *De lapide philosophico* (1625), with the comment: 'The Sea is the body; the two fish are spirit and soul.'

to other people no matter how far apart. Pisces is too diffuse to be contained or defined by the ego. Rather, it describes the place in the birth chart where we lose ourselves and surrender our own personal willpower and direction in life. With so much going on psychically, there is often a curious lack of engagement with, or commitment to, personal relationships, which I think is a feature of the non-personal mutability of the sign. A Piscean student I had a while ago explained to me that although she had several children of her own, she was just as fond of her children's friends, and just as happy when they went away as when they were at home. She was perfectly happy to go with the flow and did not personally identify with any of it.

The mutability of this sign can express itself as a refusal to establish healthy boundaries or to take any kind of responsibility, which can become self destructive to the point of manifesting as an addiction to vulnerability, weakness and self-sacrifice, which can be extremely masochistic. The conscious integration of Mercury, which is in detriment in Pisces, can lend analytical thinking and objectivity to the otherwise overwhelming fluidity of this sign. There are so many fleeting impressions, changing emotions and subtle influences constantly occurring for Pisceans in the psychic background, that they often don't need any additional stimulation from the world at all. Often quite the reverse. It can be very helpful for Pisceans, who have no boundaries of their own, to construct some kind of outer container or structure which will give them the privacy they need and protect them from becoming too diffuse, dispersed, overwhelmed or poisoned by their environment. This structure can be a place of escape and seclusion – any kind of bolt hole – such as a public library, or a retreat, or a weekend fishing on the banks of a river.

The Neptune ruler of Pisces describes the mystical, devotional nature of the sign. The Neptune ruler alludes to another dimension of connectedness which can be described as the part in all of us that never wanted to incarnate in the first place and longs to return to formlessness and oblivion, or to experience mystical salvation and redemption. Pisces describes a vast range of feelings, all the way from divine content to divine discontent. Neptune rules drugs and alcohol and any addictions which help us lose ourselves and escape from the world. 'Reality' is often too difficult, harsh, brutal and restrictive for Pisceans.

Planets in Pisces

Let's look at some of the planets in Pisces. Sally has Moon in Pisces. This is an extremely impressionable and imaginative placement, describing Sally's need (Moon) to merge with something greater than herself (Pisces). There will be a powerful symbiotic relationship and/or strong psychic connection with her mother, which can be extremely supportive and nurturing on one hand and emotionally demanding on the other – very often both. If the Moon describes what we need and what feeds us, the Moon in Pisces can indicate that there are no boundaries or limits to our neediness. We may never feel safe. The result can be that we are forever hungry and thirsty, feeling that our needs can never be fulfilled or satisfied, which can result in addictive tendencies. It is also possible to find that we end up driving others away, since they can become overwhelmed or feel 'drowned' by our neediness. On the other hand, if the Moon in Pisces can be diverted away from the battleground of the ego's demands for safety and security, it ultimately describes a strong and loving connection to one's own soul and can indeed find fulfillment in unconditional devotion to something greater than oneself.

If you have Mercury in Pisces, then you know that everything is relative and that the truth can be anything you want it to be. If you want black to be white, then that is fine. Mercury in Pisces can cast a spell, spin a tale, promote a sale, and communicate in a variety of non verbal ways, such as through mime, music, dance and art. Mercury in Pisces has a vivid and poetic imagination, sensitive to the feel and atmosphere of words rather than to their actual concrete meaning. It can also describe confused thinking and invasive thoughts.

Audience: This is an interesting way of looking at it, because my son has Mercury in Pisces and he will tell you whatever he thinks you want to hear. It drives me mad, because as far as I am concerned he is lying.

Clare: Well, you will often read that Mercury in Pisces can be dishonest. And indeed, from a factual earth or air point of view, this may be the case. But from your son's point of view, he is more likely to respond to you on an emotional level, and try to protect you or try to avoid making a commitment by telling you what you want to hear. As a passive collective sign, it is also very likely that he doesn't know what he thinks and so any one answer may be as good as any other answer.

Audience: So you mean that the lights are on, but there's nobody home?

Clare: Not so much that there is nobody at home, but rather that the Piscean is unable or unwilling to discriminate, so you can have whichever piece of it you would like, since it doesn't matter either way. The television impersonator Rory Bremner, who has Mercury in Pisces, can 'become' whoever he is impersonating, even to the extent that he appears to take on their shape as well as their voice and mannerisms. He can feel his way into becoming a certain person, which will be much easier for him than being himself, which he may not be so clear about.

Audience: I have Sun, Mercury and Ascendant in Pisces and I can certainly relate to what you are saying.

Clare: Yes, and of course we all have the sign of Pisces and the planet Neptune in our charts, so we all have places where we long to surrender and to some extent we should all be able to relate to these themes.

David has Venus in Pisces, which indicates a pronounced sensitivity to and appreciation of music, dance, art, fantasy, film, fashion and romance. Venus in Pisces can describe a person in love with the ideal of love, someone with the capacity for unconditional love and devotion to others, to the extent that it is not personal. On a personal level, it can also describe dissatisfaction or disappointment or deception in relationships.

Chiron in Pisces often describes a kind of 'existential loneliness', a feeling of being cut off from the source of support, a kind of emotional exile, which people will often spend many years trying to heal through relationships. It is as if Pisces holds a memory of oneness with everything, which may be a memory of mystical connection or a memory of life in the womb. Eventually, we can come to accept that, for so long as we are in separate bodies this kind of loneliness is an intrinsic part of the human condition, and therefore something that we all feel at some level. Once we have accepted that the umbilical cord has been cut, we can develop compassion for ourselves and others since, to some extent, we all feel this existential wound.

In the end, Pisces has a vast range of expressions. As the last sign of the zodiac it is about surrendering and letting go, dissolving into a greater whole and preparing for a new beginning and a new life when Pisces gives way once again to Aries and the great story starts to unfold again. On that point I think we can all drift home! Have a wonderful holiday and I look forward to seeing you all again next term.

Bibliography

Baring, A. & Cashford, J.	(1991)	*The Myth of the Goddess*, Penguin/Arkana
Buber, M.	(1938)	*I and Thou*, T. & T. Clark Ltd.
Campion, N.	(1994)	*The Great Year: Astrology, Millenarianism and History in the Western Tradition*, Penguin/Arkana
Collin, R.	(1968)	*The Theory of Celestial Influence: Man, the Universe and Cosmic Mystery*, Shambhala Publications, Inc.
Dethlefsen, T.	(1984)	*The Challenge of Fate*, Coventure Ltd
Edinger, E. F.	(1985)	*Anatomy of the Psyche: Alchemical Symbolism in Psychotherapy*, Open Court Publishing
	(1995)	*The Mysterium Lectures: A Journey through C.G. Jung's Mysterium Coniunctionis*, Inner City Books
Ferrucci, P.	(1982)	*What We May Be*, Jeremy Tarcher and Turnstone Press
Greene, L. & Sasportas, H.	(1987)	'Subpersonalities and Psychological Conflicts' in *The Development of the Personality*, Seminars in Psychological Astrology, Vol. 1, Samuel Weiser, Inc.
Jung, C.G.	(1983)	*Memories, Dreams and Reflections*, Fontana Paperbacks
	(1923)	*Psychological Types*, CW4, Routledge & Kegan Paul
	(1960)	'Synchronicity: An Acausal Connecting Principle', in *The Structure and Dynamics of the Psyche*, CW8, Routledge & Kegan Paul
	(1963)	*Psychology and Alchemy*, CW12, Routledge & Kegan Paul
	(1958)	*Psychology and Religion*, CW11, Routledge & Kegan Paul

	(1953)	*Mysterium Coniunctionis*, CW14, Routledge & Kegan Paul
	(1954)	'The Psychology of the Transference', in *The Practice of Psychotherapy*, CW16, Routledge & Kegan Paul
Kenton, W. (Z'ev ben Shimon Halevi)	(1985)	*The Anatomy of Fate: Kabbalistic Astrology*, Gateway Books
	(1986)	*Kabbalah and Psychology*, Gateway Books
	(1979)	*Kabbalah: Tradition of Hidden Knowledge*, Thames and Hudson
Kirschenbaum, H. & Henderson, V. L. (eds.)	(1990)	*Carl Rogers Dialogues*, Constable Press
Lash, J.	(1999)	*Quest for the Zodiac: The Cosmic Code Beyond Astrology*, Thoth Publications
Matthews, C.	(2002)	*Singing the Soul Back Home: Shamanic Wisdom for Every Day*, Connections Book Publishing
McGuire, W. & Hull, R. F. C. (eds.)	(1977)	*C.G. Jung Speaking*, Princeton University Press
Moore, T. (ed.)	(1989)	*A Blue Fire: The Essential James Hillman*, Routledge
Moore, T.	(1997)	*The Re-Enchantment of Everyday Life*, Harper Perennial
Nicoll, M.	(1985)	*Psychological Commentaries on the Teaching of Gurdjieff and Ouspensky*, Vol. 1 Shambhala Publications, Inc.
Reinhart, M.	(1989)	*Chiron and the Healing Journey: An Astrological and Psychological Perspective*, Penguin/Arkana
	(1996)	*To the Edge and Beyond: Saturn, Chiron, Pholus and the Centaurs*, CPA Press
Roberts, J. M.	(1992)	*A History of the World*, Helicon Publishing Ltd.
Schwartz-Salant, N. (ed.)	(1995)	*C.G. Jung: Jung on Alchemy*, Routledge

Von Franz, M-L.	(1975)	*C.G. Jung: His Myth in Our Time*, C.G. Jung Foundation for Analytical Psychology, Inc.
West, J. A.	(1979)	*Serpent in the Sky: The High Wisdom of Ancient Egypt*, The Julian Press, Inc.
Whitmont, E. C.	(1978)	*The Symbolic Quest: Basic Concepts of Analytical Psychology*, Princeton University Press
Wilber, Ken	(1998)	*The Eye of Spirit: An Integral Vision for a World Gone Slightly Mad*, Shambhala Publications, Inc.
Yates, F.A.	(1964)	*Giordano Bruno and the Hermetic Tradition*, University of Chicago Press

Recommended Reading List

Planets

The Inner Planets

Bell, L., Costello, D., Greene, L., Reinhart, M.	(2001)	*The Mars Quartet: Four Seminars on the Astrology of the Red Planet*, London: CPA Press
Costello, D.	(2003)	*The Astrological Moon*, London: CPA Press
Greene, L.	(2001)	*Apollo's Chariot: The Meaning of the Astrological Sun*, London: CPA Press
Greene, L. & Sasportas, H.	(1993)	*The Inner Planets: Building Blocks of Personal Reality*, Seminars in Psychological Astrology, Vol. 4, York Beach, ME: Samuel Weiser, Inc.
	(1992)	*The Luminaries: The Psychology of the Sun and Moon in the Horoscope*, Seminars in Psychological Astrology, Vol. 3, York Beach, ME: Samuel Weiser, Inc.
Harvey, C.	(2005)	*Mercury the Translator* (Studyshop on CD), London: Astro Logos Ltd.
Harvey, C. & Harvey, S.	(1994)	*Sun Sign, Moon Sign*, London: HarperCollins

Moore, M.	(1990)	*The Planets Within: The Astrological Psychology of Marsilio Ficino*, Great Barrington, MA: Lindisfarne Press

Jupiter and Saturn

Greene, L.	(1976)	*Saturn: A New Look At an Old Devil*, York Beach, ME: Samuel Weiser, Inc.
Greene, L. & Arroyo, S.	(1984)	*The Jupiter/Saturn Conference Lectures* (later published as *New Insights in Modern Astrology*, 1991), Sebastopol, CA: , CRCS Publications

The Outer Planets

Greene, L.	(1996)	*The Art of Stealing Fire: Uranus in the Horoscope*, London: CPA Press
	(1996)	*The Astrological Neptune and the Quest for Redemption*, York Beach, ME: Samuel Weiser, Inc.
	(2004)	*The Astrology of Fate*, York Beach, ME: Red Wheel/Weiser,
	(2005)	*Neptune* (Studyshop on CD), London: Astro Logos Ltd.
	(2005)	*The Outer Planets and Their Cycles: The Astrology of the Collective*, London: CPA Press
	(2005)	*Pluto and the Inner Planets* (Studyshop on CD), London: Astro Logos Ltd.
Reinhart, M.	(1989)	*Chiron and the Healing Journey*, London: Penguin/Arkana
	(1996)	*Saturn, Chiron and the Centaurs: To the Edge and Beyond*, London: CPA Press
Sasportas, H.	(2007)	*The Gods of Change: Pain, Crisis and the Transits of Uranus, Neptune and Pluto*, Bournemouth: The Wessex Astrologer
Tarnas, R.	(1995)	*Prometheus the Awakener: An Essay on the Archetypal Meaning of the Planet Uranus*, Oxford: Auriel Press

The Signs and Elements

Arroyo, S.	(1975)	*Astrology, Psychology and the Four Elements*, Reno, NE: CRCS Publications
Costello, D.	(1998)	*Water and Fire*, London: CPA Press
	(1999)	*Earth and Air*, London: CPA Press
Greene, L.	(1986)	*Astrology for Lovers*, York Beach, ME: Samuel Weiser, Inc.
	(1996)	*Barriers and Boundaries: The Horoscope and the Defences of the Personality*, London: CPA Press

General

Greene, L.	(1978)	*Relating*, York Beach, ME: Samuel Weiser, Inc.
Greene L. & Sasportas, H.	(1987)	*The Development of the Personality*, Seminars in Psychological Astrology, Vol. 1, York Beach, ME: Samuel Weiser, Inc.
	(1988)	*Dynamics of the Unconscious*, Seminars in Psychological Astrology, Vol. 2, York Beach, ME: Samuel Weiser, Inc.

About the Centre for Psychological Astrology

The Centre for Psychological Astrology was founded in 1983 by Dr Liz Greene and Howard Sasportas. Since its inception, the CPA has become world renowned for its unique and inspiring application of a variety of psychological approaches to astrology.

The Centre continues to foster the cross-fertilisation of the fields of astrology and depth, humanistic and transpersonal psychology. It hosts a unique seminar and webinar programme providing an original, informal and inspiring framework for both beginners and experienced astrologers. Past seminars are available as books and e-books through the CPA Press.

For further information about the current programme of seminars and webinars, to receive mailings and browse the CPA Press astrology books, contact the Administrator, Juliet Sharman-Burke at: juliet@cpalondon.com

The **Online Introductory Certificate Course** with John Green provides a foundation in the basics of psychological astrology. Run as real time online tutorials, students can interact with the tutor and other students, ask questions and watch recorded sessions.

For further information, contact John at: webmaster@cpalondon.com

About the Mercury Internet School of Psychological Astrology

The Mercury Internet School of Psychological Astrology (MISPA) offers a Diploma Course, and students who have completed the CPA's Foundation Course are eligible to enrol.

For further information visit: www.mercuryinternetschool.com or write to info@mercuryinternetschool.com

About the Faculty of Astrological Studies

The Faculty of Astrological Studies was founded in London to raise the standard of astrological education. The Faculty remains at the forefront of the serious teaching of astrology, preserving the links to this ancient craft, embracing new developments and passing on this knowledge to students all over the world.

Since its foundation in 1948, the Faculty has become known worldwide as a first class astrological school, and more than 10,000 students from over 90 countries have enrolled on its courses. Its Diploma is among the most highly valued and recognised international qualifications for the professional astrologer. Many of the world's leading astrologers are or were Faculty Diploma holders, such as Dr Liz Greene, Charles Harvey, Julia Parker, Melanie Reinhart and Howard Sasportas.

The Faculty's team of dedicated tutors, all of whom are themselves Faculty Diploma holders, are devoted to teaching astrology to students all over the world, guiding them carefully from the very beginning of their astrological studies right through to professional qualification at Diploma level. The Faculty's courses are comprehensive and flexible, available online and at classes and seminars in London. Full and part Diploma modules can also be studied at the Faculty's annual Oxford Summer School. Students can choose whichever method of learning suits them best, and alternate freely between them to suit their individual circumstances.

The Faculty's course material is unique, with a philosophical but practical approach to the art and craft of astrology, preserving its rich traditions and at the same time embracing and including modern psychological and post-psychological thinking. Course material is constantly updated, providing students with thorough, in-depth and comprehensive guidance, supported by their own personal tutor.

For further information visit: www.astrology.org.uk or write to: info@astrology.org.uk

www.ingramcontent.com/pod-product-compliance
Lightning Source LLC
Chambersburg PA
CBHW061939220426
43662CB00012B/1960